Artificial Intelligence
for Security

Other books by Archie Addo published by Business Expert Press

Artificial Intelligence Design and Solution for Risk and Security
ISBN: 9781951527488
https://www.businessexpertpress.com/books/artificial-intelligence-
design-and-solution-for-risk-and-security/

Artificial Intelligence for Risk Management
ISBN: 9781949443516
https://www.businessexpertpress.com/books/artificial-intelligence-for-
risk-management/

Artificial Intelligence for Security

Archie Addo, Srini Centhala, and
Muthu Shanmugam

BEP BUSINESS EXPERT PRESS

Artificial Intelligence for Security

First published in 2020 by
Business Expert Press, LLC
222 East 46th Street, New York, NY 10017
www.businessexpertpress.com

ISBN-13: 978-1-95152-726-6 (paperback)
ISBN-13: 978-1-95152-727-3 (e-book)

Business Expert Press Business Law and Corporate Risk Management Collection

Collection ISSN: 2333-6722 (print)
Collection ISSN: 2333-6730 (electronic)

Cover and interior design by Exeter Premedia Services Private Ltd., Chennai, India

First edition: 2020

10 9 8 7 6 5 4 3 2 1

Printed in the United States of America.

Abstract

Shootings are becoming prevalent in the United States (Lankford, Adkins, and Madfis 2019). Oftentimes, shooters post their intentions on the Internet before carrying out the act of shooting. Security organizations plant bots to help trace postings that could lead to harm.

The bots—also known as botnet—help organizations to avoid harmful security situations (Anzilotti et al. 2019; Berinato 2018). Other approaches can be used to identify security issues early enough to avoid harmful situations and minimize impact. Security management plays a major role in the case of uncertainty. Security management must ask the following questions: How can this situation be forecasted and managed? Can the occurrences be captured historically? Can such patterns of occurrences be identified? Can the data relating to the occurrences be captured? Can the data be used to predict future occurrences? Can the relevance of the data be an important factor? Does the security piece become important? What happens if the data are manipulated? How is the data manipulated? How can the data be protected and saved safely? Security plays an important role with data and is considered a driving factor in security management.

Various types of securities apply to certain industries, business functions, roles, and responsibilities (Clark 2019). This book intends to illustrate the top security business cases and use cases that apply to respective industries by defining, analyzing, monitoring, controlling, and mitigating the associated securities.

It is important to use the data and put corrective actions in place to observe lurking security. The empirical study shows that large amounts of data take a long time to process and cannot be analyzed by a human. Data science, data analytics, and machine learning (ML) algorithms can be used (De Veaux and De Veaux 2019; Hao and Ho 2019).

Artificial intelligence (AI) enables machines to learn from previous human experiences and enables continuous learning from new sets of input data. The development of mathematical algorithms has led to the creation of ML and subsequently to the AI revolution.

AI is used to determine how security should be approached. AI produces effective and dramatic results in business and can aid organizations in understanding and improving security management skills.

Security has become important everywhere due to the large volume of data, different velocities, and variety of data. These rationales are growing and are used more frequently with any amount of negative impact. The range and breadth of security creates havoc everywhere in the world on a variety of projects. Security management is important in an organization; without it, an organization may struggle with defining its objectives. Data security strategies are important in many ways; however, the most important strategical implementation is to avoid financial loss. This book focuses on problem statements with appropriate use cases and proposes AI solutions using data science and ML approaches.

This book aims to give concrete answers to the following crucial questions: Where are these securities and what can be done to lower the impacts? Is AI part of the answer to security mitigation?

Keywords

project management; construction management; program management; skills development; security; artificial intelligence; analytics; ML; mitigation; performance review; data science and business intelligence

Contents

Acknowledgments...ix

Chapter 1   Introduction...1
Chapter 2   Introduction to Security 5
Chapter 3   How AI and Security Come Together?..............57
Chapter 4   Knowledgebase...65
Chapter 5   AI Solutions for Security.................................69
Chapter 6   Industry Domain..109
Chapter 7   Conclusion..127

References...129
About the Authors..133
Index 135

Acknowledgments

Our artificial intelligence (AI) and security expert colleagues have worked in the international corporate world to acquire knowledge and expertise. AI and security researchers and practitioners have had a profound impact on our thinking and on the contents of this book. Subsequently, working with many corporate customers has greatly influenced the preparation of this material.

Thank you to our parents, Godson Addo, Mary (Vanderpuije) Addo, Seetharaman Centhala, Thulasi Centhala, K. Shanmugam, and S. Saroja, for encouraging us to get an education and work diligently in our field. We do not think we would have made it this far without their support.

We would like to extend great thanks to our families: Louvaine Addo, Mala Srini, and Kavitha Muthu; Archie and Srini's children: Koushik Seethula, Shashank Seethula, and Srima Seethula; and Muthu's children: Maanasa Muthu and Sarvesh Muthu for their collective patience with our busy schedules.

Thank you to Editide for copyediting. We would like to extend great thanks to Venkat and everyone at Bizstats Technologies Pvt. Ltd. who enabled us to be Software-as-a-Service (SaaS) BizStats AI company, which provided major input for this book.

CHAPTER 1

Introduction

- Target Audience
- What Do You Get from the Book?
- What This Book Covers
- This Book's Mind Map
- Organization of Chapters
  - o Introduction to Security
  - o Introduction to the AI Knowledge Base
  - o How AI Security Comes Together
  - o Business Use Cases
  - o AI Solutions for Security
  - o Industry Domain
- Conclusion
- References

Chapter Outline

- Book introduction
- Organization of the book
- Chapter introduction

Key Learning Points

- Learn and understand the introduction

Target Audience

This book mainly focuses on how artificial intelligence (AI) can be applied to security management. This book follows current trends of AI in the branches of natural language processing, natural language question and answering systems, conversational AI (Reddy 2018) in security domains, AI supporting drones, AI cybersecurity, Internet of things (IoT) devices, and use cases.

Applicable AI topics target the following groups:

- Corporate top executives, founders, chief technology officers, chief information officers, chief data officers, chief security officers, data scientists, data architects, AI designers, AI engineers, project managers, and consultants to understand how to manage security using AI.
- Students, teachers, and developers will find this book useful and practical. It will provide an overview of many AI components and introduce how AI can be used in corporate environments and start-up companies.
- Anybody who strives to understand how AI can be used for security.

What Do You Get from the Book?

- Understand and learn about AI and how to apply AI to security.
- Design and apply knowledge-based AI solutions to solve security problems.
- The design of AI applied systems relies primarily on the following:
  o Subject Matter Experts. This means having a practical view of how solutions can be used. In this book, security is used as an example with case studies.
  o Appropriately applied mathematics and algorithms are used in the book. Do not skip the mathematical equations if you have the need to study them. It is important to note that AI relies heavily on mathematics.
  o Applied physics and usage in hardware systems and futuristic approaches from quantum computers to parallel processing of the quantum computer handling network. AI

is evolving into a new era of possible opportunities. New concepts and applied creative ideas are introduced in the futuristic AI chapter.

- Decision theory, decision-making processes, the Markov decision process, and algorithms.

What This Book Covers

This book introduces AI and explains how AI is applied to corporations, start-ups, and companies of all sizes to help automate the tedious job of maintaining security. AI and machine learning can automate the working environment of an organization, thus creating resources for organizational employees. The following questions are addressed in this book.

- How do I get true value from AI?
- What is the business use cases for AI with visionary?

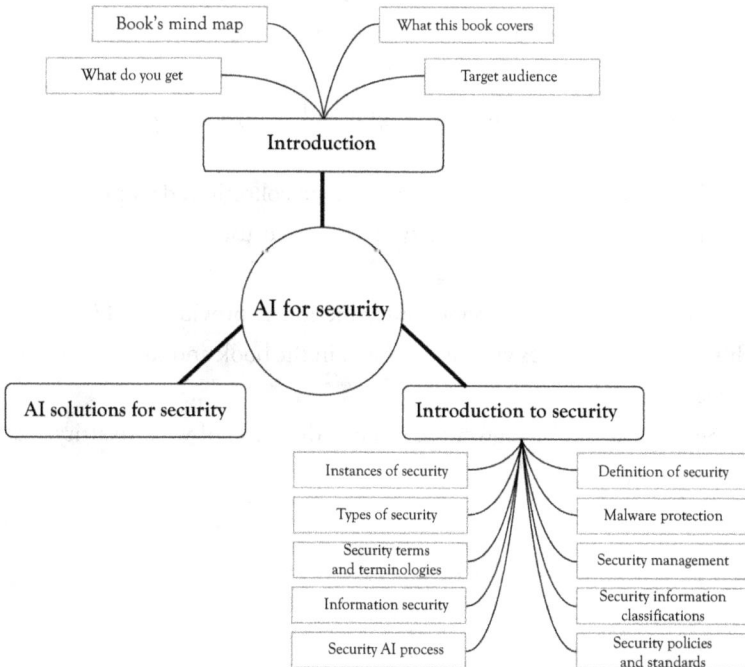

Figure 1.1 Mind map of the book

Firms in AI cybersecurity

Security AI process

Asset Discovery

Intrusion detection

Endpoint
detection and response

Discover AI

Monitor AI

AI
Solutions
for security

Detect AI

Monitor in
discover phase

Monitor in
detect phase

Monitor in threat
scoring phase

Monitor in threat
response phase

Moniter in
pretect phase

Threat score AI

Protect AI

Threat response AI

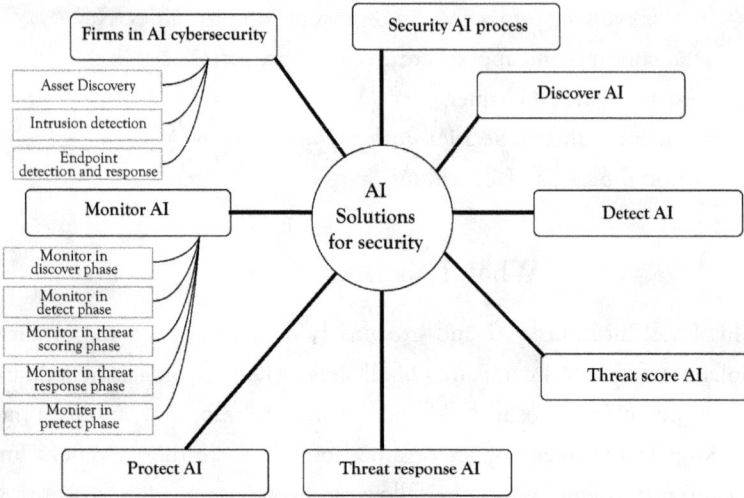

Figure 1.2 Mind map of AI solutions for security

- How do I identify the best business case for AI adoption and evaluate opportunities?
- Should I build or buy an AI platform?
- How do I find and recruit top AI talent for my enterprise?
- How will I bring AI into my business to increase revenue or decrease costs?
- How can I facilitate AI adoption within my organization?

This book addresses how to manage data collection, data preparation, data transformation, data security, and how to use the data to align AI use case.

A mind map for the book's introduction is provided in Figure 1.1. This figure summarizes what is discussed in the book and the organization of chapters.

See Figure 1.2. This gives the reader a direction of what security areas are covered with AI solutions.

CHAPTER 2

Introduction to Security

- Definition of Security
- By Example: Security Business Case
- Different Types of Security
- Security Management Process

Chapter Outline
- Define security and provide examples
- Illustrate various security areas
- Illustrate security process areas in detail
- Determine security mitigations
- Illustrate security standards

Key Learning Points
- Learn and understand security
- Identify security areas
- Mitigate security issues
- Understand what security uncertainties exist
- Analyzing and determining which security events must have a planned response
- Adopting approaches to each security event and defining what triggers a response
- Maintaining security plans
- Monitoring security occurrences

Definition of Security

Security is defined as the act of protecting the contents of something. Security has been in existence for many years (Mishchuk 2018) and protects organizations from destruction, modification, and unauthorized access. Security protects any resources through any medium. Various areas such as the environment, physical, health, national, economic, and energy all require security.

- *Environmental security:* The protection against the changing climate through air conditioning in the summer or using the heater in the winter is an example of environmental security.
- *Physical security:* Airport security is a kind of physical security.
- *Cybersecurity:* Cybersecurity consists of protection of data information by using different types of authentication.
- *Health security:* The use of a flu shot to protect against flu is an example of health security.

An organization must be protected from computer security threats. A security policy is an outline of how threats should be handled during an attack. Nearly all organizations base their security policies on the organization's specific field. Cyberterrorism can be defined as a motivated attack against computer security, computer programs, and information, which can be used against people's will. An example of cyberterrorism is the attack at J.P. Morgan Chase in 2012 (Berger, Imbierowicz, and Rauch 2016). The J.P. Morgan security group failed to convey two-factor authentication on one of the organization's numerous servers, prompting the nonappearance of a security layer that may have generally stopped the attack. This compromised 90 servers and 83,000,000 accounts. The Federal Information Security Management Act (FISMA) and the Health Insurance Portability and Accountability Act (HIPAA) are different types of security that ensure privacy protection of the data and enhance national security.

Business Challenges

Business challenges vary depending on the domain. The following security mitigations are used in these specific domains (Umasuthan 2016; Kastner, Hu, and Althoff 2016):

1. User domains: Every organization has their own security policies as per their business requirement. Security issues make each employee aware of their organization's policies. This can be mitigated through awareness, enforcement, rewards, and monitoring.
2. Workstations: Hackers can use workstations to breach the internal network of an organization. Robust security policies help in establish a vigorous automated patch management process.
3. Local area network domains: Local area networks include desktops, laptops, mobile devices, and Internet of things (IoT) devices. Sensors are used in marketing, health sectors, and communication sectors to enhance productivity, collaboration, and responsiveness. A superior security policy should be instilled in the firewall to restrict unwanted videos, images, files, file extensions, and data.
4. Local area networks to wide area networks: Local area networks to wide area networks protect the servers of an organization in a de-militarized zone (DMZ). Organizations are always concerned about server integrity and availability, and strong security policies set rules for restricting and monitoring traffic. Security policies also outline how servers should be configured and how security patches should be applied.
5. Wide area network domains: Organizations use a Virtual Private Network (VPN) to access the internal network through the public network. It is necessary to protect the organization's assets through an actual set of security policies in a wide area network domain, which describes how each connection type should be configured and protected. Security policies must address the vendor and validate security configurations.

Security Standards and Policies

Every organization has its own security standards. Security Standard Organizations published a specification that establishes a common language and contains rules, regulations, and definitions which should be followed by all the employees of that organization. Some of the popular security standards related to the information technology industry are as follows (Tan 2018):

- BIT financial service roundtable
- Common criteria
- ISO/IEC 27001:2013
- ISO27002:2013
- COBIT 2019

These standards are discussed in detail in further chapters. Artificial intelligence (AI) solutions for security use these industry standards as input for training machine learning (ML) models.

This book focuses on organization related to cybersecurity, such as security forces, security guard, cybersecurity systems, security cameras, and remote guarding. This discussion extends to the latest cybersecurity trends, such as IoT devices, sensors, and chatbots.

Security in Simple Terms

Security can be defined as freedom from the harm or unwanted pressure caused by people, systems, devices, sensors, or bots. Individuals, social groups, objects, institutions, ecosystems, or any other entity or phenomenon vulnerable to unwanted change may be intimidated by security.

In simple terms, security is a state of being safe, secure, and protected.

- IT security is a strategy that prevents unauthorized access to organizations or IT industries' assets such as computers, networks, and data. IT security protects the confidentiality of sensitive information and blocks the access of sophisticated hackers.
- Information security is a set of strategies that manages the processes, tools, and policies necessary to prevent, detect, document, and counter threats to digital and nondigital information.

Information Security

Recently, information security has created a buzz in the IT field (Stafford, Deitz, and Li 2018).

Information security accountabilities include forming a set of business procedures to defend information assets regardless of how the information is formatted or whether the information is in transit, being processed, or being stored. Information security programs are built around the Central Intelligence Agency's core objectives: to maintain the confidentiality, integrity, and availability of IT systems and business data. These objectives ensure that sensitive information is only disclosed to authorized parties, prevents unauthorized modification of data, and guarantees the data can be accessed by authorized parties when requested.

Many large organizations make a conscious effort to use standard security gathering to accomplish and maintain the association's information security program. The main data security officer leads this effort. Most organizations conduct security management: a procedure that evaluates vulnerabilities and dangers to data resources and connects the proper defensive controls. The estimation of an association exists in its data and requires basic security for business tasks.

Data security requires procedures and arrangements to regulate security maintenance. This maintenance includes physical and computerized safety efforts to protect information from unapproved access, use, replication, or eradication. These requirements can incorporate mantraps and encryption key administration and organize interruption identification frameworks, secret key approaches, and administrative consistency. A security review will be conducted to assess the organization's capacity to use secure frameworks against possible security issues.

Security threats come in a wide range of formats and structures (InfoSec 2018); typically, these threats involve malware, phishing attacks, fraud, and ransomware. Numerous security controls compose a layered barrier using a top to bottom procedure to stop attackers and alleviate vulnerabilities in different areas. This strategy reduces the effect of an assault. Security gatherings should have a reaction plan set up; this enables the organization to contain and restrain harm, expel the threat, and introduce new security ideas and controls.

The following are the different types of information security:

- *Application security:* Application security is a broad topic that covers software vulnerabilities in web and mobile applications and application programming interfaces. These vulnerabilities may be found in authentication or authorization of users, the integrity of code and configurations, and mature policies and procedures. Application vulnerabilities can create entry points for significant information security breaches. Application security is an important part of perimeter defense.

- *Cloud security:* Cloud security focuses on building and hosting secure applications in Cloud environments and securely consuming third-party Cloud applications. The term "Cloud" simply means that the application is running in a shared environment. Businesses must ensure adequate isolation between different processes in shared environments.
- *Infrastructure security:* Infrastructure security deals with the protection of internal and extranet networks, labs, data centers, servers, desktops, and mobile devices.
- *Vulnerability management:* Vulnerability management is the process of scanning an environment for weak points (such as unpatched software) and prioritizing remediation based on security issues.
- *Cybersecurity:* Cybersecurity is the practice of protecting systems, networks, and programs from digital attacks.

Security Terms and Terminologies

Here are some of the important terms used in the security business area (Barylick 2019).

Malware (or virus): Malware is malicious software designed to cause harm, gain unauthorized access to any computer systems, and corrupt data. Malware invades devices such as computer systems, networks, tablets, and mobile devices. It has the capability to take partial control of the device and creates havoc by destroying the normal function of the device. Malware does not have the potential to destroy the physical component of the device; however, it can steal, encrypt, or delete the data. It can also alter the computer's core functions and spy on the device activity without the owner's knowledge or permission. Malware can affect the connection to the Internet and can download software and applications from unknown websites.

Other forms of malware are:

- *Adware* is designed to display advertisements on the computer screen. This annoys the user and is usually linked with other applications.
- A *virus* is a type of malware that links with another program or application. When a program is run, viruses can reproduce themselves by the changing program being run.
- *Spyware* is a malware that is installed on a computer without the owner's permission. The purpose of this virus is to collect information on the victim's computer. This could be due to espionage or simply act as a key logger. Users can activate spyware by carelessly accepting a prompt or pop-up without reading it first, downloading software from an unreliable source, accepting e-mails from unknown senders, and copying movies, music, or games. It is a good idea to run antivirus software to remove the suspected software if one suspects spyware activity. Follow these steps to prevent spyware from being installed:
  o Only open e-mails from senders you know.
  o Restrict downloads from reliable sources.
  o Avoid clicking on pop-up advertisements.
  o Install reliable and proven antivirus computer devices.
- *Worms* are a virus that is self-replicating and spreads in the device hosting it. Worm self-replicating happens in the network the device is linked with. The idea is to destroy files and data on the network.
- *Trojan and Trojan Horse* is the most dangerous type of malware. It behaves as a useful item but can be dangerous. It allows the attackers to access the victim's device that to steal financial information which subsequently leads to stealing money. The Trojan can spy on the victim's computer and steal sensitive data. Trojan can also delete data, copy data, block data, and eventually disrupt the performance of the victim's

computer. Trojan does not have the ability to self-replicate. The different types of Trojans are as follows: Backdoor, Exploit, Rootkit, Banker, Trojan-DDoS, Trojan-Downloader, Trojan-Dropper, Trojan-, Fake AV, Trojan-GameThief, Trojan-Ransom, Trojan-SMS, Trojan-Spy, Trojan-Mailfinder, Trojan-Clicker, Trojan-Notifier, Trojan-Proxy, and Trojan-PSW.

- An organization can protect its computers by installing anti-malware software on servers, personal computers (PCs), laptops, Apple Macs, tablets, and smartphones. Typical anti-malware software such as Kaspersky Anti-Virus and Norton Anti-Malware can be used. Kaspersky Anti-Virus works well on android smartphones, Windows PC, Linux computers, Apple Macs, smartphones, and tablets.

- *Ransomware* is a form of malware that jams a computer device and may encrypt the files on the device, subsequently forcing the victim to pay some money. Ransomware is sometimes referred to as the cyber criminal's weapon of choice because it demands a quick, profitable payment in hard-to-trace crypto-currency. It is easy to obtain the code for ransomware through online criminal marketplaces and defending against ransom-ware is very difficult.

- *Rootkit* is a malware that provides the attacker with admin-istrator privileges on the infected device. This allows the malware to damage the device. The malware stays hidden in the device's operating system.

- *Keylogger* is a malware that tries to record the user's keystrokes on the keyboard. This malware stores stolen information and sends it to the attacker. The attacker may be looking for sensi-tive information that can be used for devious means. Typical information may consist of usernames, passwords, and credit card details.

- *Malicious cryptomining or cryptojacking* is an increasingly dominant malware planted into the computer device by a Trojan. Cryptomining allows someone else to remotely use your computer to mine cryptocurrencies such as Bitcoin and Monero. This malware allows the attacker to cash in the user's money.

- *Exploit* is a malware that takes advantage of bugs and vulnerabilities in a device with the intent to take control. Exploit is linked to malvertising: an attack through a genuine site that unknowingly pulls in content from a malicious site. Exploit installs itself on the victim's computer in a drive-by download. The victim's device is infected through visiting a website.

The following signs indicate a malware infection:

- When the device slows down for unexplained reasons, typically when browsing the Internet.
- Unusual rain of pop-up advertisements on the device screen.
- The device suddenly crashes and freezes.
- The device suddenly runs out of disk space.
- Unusually high usage of the device system that causes the device fan to start whirling at full speed.
- The sudden change of the browser homepage without the owner's permission.
- A sudden slowdown of the browser.
- The sudden additional appearance of toolbars and plugins on the browser.
- The antivirus suddenly stops working or is disabled.
- Stealthy malware called Ransome may announce that it has the data and demands money before releasing the captured files.
- Powerful malware can hide deep in the device, snag passwords, steal sensitive files, or use the device to spread the virus to other connected devices.

Removing Malware

Take the following steps if there is any suspicious of malware:

- Download anti-malware program, from:
  o https://malwarebytes.com/premium/,
  o https://malwarebytes.com/mac/,

- o https://malwarebytes.com/mobile/,
- o https://malwarebytes.com/chromebook/,
- o https://malwarebytes.com/business/.
- Install the downloaded anti-malware program and run it.
- Anti-malware finds and eliminates any malware on the device.
- Change the password and possibly the e-mail.
- Potentially use security software to screen and block scam calls and text such as Malwarebytes for iOS.
- Avoid using odd websites.

Backdoor is an intentional hole placed in the system perimeter to allow for future access that can bypass perimeter protections. Sometimes data are encrypted to bypass the customary security system. It is possible that a developer may create a backdoor to enable an application or operating system for troubleshooting or other purposes. This can be dangerous because an attacker can use the backdoor to detect or install an exploit. A worm or virus is designed to take advantage of a backdoor and will attack the device.

It is possible that encryption algorithms and networking protocols may use the backdoor; however, the backdoor can be difficult to detect. Security professionals can use specialized tools to detect backdoors or use a protocol monitoring tool to check the network packets.

To avoid backdoor attacks, avoid untrusted software and ensure that every device is protected with a firewall. An application firewall can prevent backdoor exploitation by restricting traffic.

Bot: This is a malware that allows attackers to remotely take over and control computer systems, making them behave like zombies.

Botnet: This is a network of privately infested computers with malicious software with the intent to control computers without the owners' knowledge (e.g., sending spam messages to other computers).

Exploit: This is a malware that uses software codes to exploit specific vulnerabilities in other software applications or frameworks that can be a dangerous adversary effort.

Scanning: Scanning makes frequent requests to access computers. This can be in the form of brute-force. The intent is to find weak points and vulnerability and collect information.

Sniffing: This is a malware that observes and records network and in-server traffic and processes the information without the knowledge of network operators.

Keylogger: This is a software that records the keys pressed on a keyboard or similar computer input device.

Spam: Spam solicits messages for the purposes of advertising. Usually, spam come in the form of e-mails, but it can also be in the form of text messages.

Login attack: The attacks are automating attempts of guessing credentials for automation systems; this could be in the form of a brute-force attack.

Account takeover: This is an attempt to gain access to an account that does not belong to the perpetrator. Often, this leads to identity theft, stealing money, spyware installation, and social engineering.

Phishing (aka *masquerading*): This is a software that pretends to be someone with the intent to induce the revelation of personal information or to obtain private assets.

Spear phishing: This targets a user with the intent of making use of the user's confidential information.

Social engineering: This is the extraction of information from humans using nontechnical methods such as trickery and lying.

Incendiary speech: This is harmful speech targeted at individual people or groups.

Denial of service and *distributed denial of service:* This is the attack of systems that do not have much security or protection. This is done through high-volume bombardments or malformed requests.

Advanced persistent threats: This is a brute-force attack toward a network or host where the intruder remains undetected for a long period of time. The intent is to steal data and penetrate the system for an intended purpose.

Zero-day vulnerability: This plants a subtle bug in a computer system that remains a weak link to the system. This bug is used for potential exploitation until the vendor comes out with a patch for the system. Usually, the vendor is not aware of the problem for some time.

Why ML and AI for Security Area?

People use the Internet to provide free transmission and broad distribution of textual, video, and image materials. This has led to the widespread advertisement of commercial and noncommercial items. Subsequently, the Internet has led to accounts being stolen and the spreading of viruses, worms, Trojans, and so on. Spam interrupts Internet users daily. This constant interruption is a bother to many people and corporations.

ML and AI help detect malware, viruses, Trojans, and all other security threats. An automated system is needed to detect and protect from these threats. Typically, the identification, detection, and protection of these problems is handled manually.

Data can be used to improve the use of technology and detect and defeat malicious adversaries. This reiterates the importance of using data and ML in the field of computer security. Almost all organizations use computers; this raises the real need to find a way to prevent adversaries that can cause security headaches. A battle exists between adversary attackers and defenders in the field of computer security; this includes spam and hacking. Each side tends to exploit or fix the flaws in design or technique. This is a constant battle that has not changed over time. Data are being increased daily due to the billions of users from across the world. This leads to a need for more powerful data analysis, which are created using ML algorithms.

ML and data analysis techniques can address problem domains in security and abuse in organizations. Suitability of different ML techniques and scenarios will be discussed. Your adversaries do not want you to use ML.

The adversary to your organization will use ML simply to hurt your business. It helps to learn how to deal with the adversary attacker when they come to you. Vigilance will help you coin the appropriate countermeasures when needed.

Adversaries use ML to speed up the process of finding vulnerabilities in software. Adversaries also use ML to discover an individual's interests through social media to send phishing messages to that individual.

It is important to remember that attackers target ML systems with erroneous algorithms, which causes false predictions and inaccurate learning. Often, ML algorithms are not designed with security in mind; adversary attempts target these algorithms. Incorporating securities approaches can help cut down on adversarial attacks on ML systems.

ML can be used for security solutions; however, ML and data science are not straightforward solutions. The detailed way to apply ML and AI is discussed in Chapter 5.

Anomaly detection targets specific learning patterns that occur inside certain subsets of the data. This establishes a normality that describes 95 percent or more of the dataset. Using this approach, deviations from this normality will be detected as anomalies. Patterns extracted through pattern recognition must be strictly derived from the observed data. On the other hand, an infinite number of anomalous patterns can fit into the dataset. Spam detection can be looked at as pattern detection. This enables an algorithm to recognize spam characteristics, usually in the case of e-mail spam. Typically, malware and botnet detection fall in the category of pattern recognition. If the threat is known, it is better to use a pattern recognition approach to detect it. Anomaly detection approach is suitable if the threat is unclear (e.g., network traffic flow with malicious network activities).

An ML approach has been used as the first defense against breaches and information theft. Subsequently, ML has been used for access control issues because of the pains imposed by rigid control policies. Unsupervised learning and anomaly detection can deduce where users fall into retaliatory action by detecting unconventional patterns. A typical example is when cross-staff correlation is required by an organization.

By Example: Security Business Case

- In simple terms, security is nothing but being free from danger or fear. A good example is national border security. Border security is related to wars between countries and can also refer to the police, who protects the masses from attacks.
- The best example of IT security is ransomware, which is a data breach. Ransomware is a type of malware. Malware is intrusive software that is designed to damage and destroy computers and computer systems. Examples of common malware include viruses, worms, Trojan viruses, spyware, adware, and ransomware.

- The best example of a data breach is the Wannacry attack on Equifax and Uber, which affected millions of consumers and thousands of business.

Different Types of Security

Physical security is defined as personnel security, communication security, and information security (Wang, Wang, and Yen 2019). This includes the protection of personnel, hardware, software, networks, and data from physical actions and events that could cause serious damage to an enterprise, agency, or institution. This includes protection from fire, flood, natural disasters, burglary, theft, vandalism, and terrorism.

Personnel Security: Personnel security is a system of policies and procedures that mitigate the security of workers (insiders), exploiting their legitimate access to an organization's assets for unauthorized purposes.

Communication security: Communication security is the prevention of unauthorized access to telecommunications traffic or to any written information that is transmitted or transferred. Communication security has several disciplines:

- Cryptographic security encrypts data and renders it unreadable until the data are decrypted.
- Emission security prevents the release or capture of equipment emanations to prevent information from unauthorized interception.
- Physical security ensures the safety of and prevents unauthorized access to a network's cryptographic information, documents, and equipment.
- Transmission security protects unauthorized access when data are physically transferred to prevent issues such as service interruption.

Network security: Network security consists of the policies and practices adopted to prevent and monitor unauthorized access, misuse, modification, or denial of a computer network and network-accessible resources. Network security involves the authorization of access to data in a network, which is controlled by the network administrator. Users choose or are assigned an ID and password or other authenticating information that allows them to access information and programs within their authority. Network security covers a variety of public and private computer networks that are used in everyday jobs. These networks conduct transactions and communications among businesses, government agencies, and individuals. Networks can be private and others might be open to public access. Network security is involved in organizations, enterprises, and other types of institutions. It does as its title explains: secures the network and protects and overseas operations. The most common and simple way of protecting a network resource is by assigning it a unique name and a corresponding password.

- *Physical security:* Physical security is the protection of personnel, hardware, software, networks, and data from physical actions, intrusions, and other events that could damage an organization. This includes natural disasters, fire, theft, and terrorism, among others. Physical security for enterprises often includes employee access control to the office buildings as well as specific locations, such as data centers.
- *Information security:* Information security—frequently referred as InfoSec—encapsulates a broad set of strategies for managing the process. These tools and policies aim to prevent, detect, and respond to threats to both digital and nondigital information assets.
- *Application security:* Application security is the protection of applications from threats that seek to manipulate application and access, steal, modify, or delete data. These protections— often caused countermeasures—use software, hardware, and policies.
- *Cloud security:* Cloud security is a set of policies and technologies designed to protect data and infrastructure involved in a Cloud computing environment. Cloud security addresses identity and access management, along with data privacy.
- *Mobile security:* Mobile security is the protection of portable devices, such as smartphones, tablets, and laptops. Mobile

security is also known as wireless security. Mobile security secures the devices and the networks they connect to in order to prevent theft, data leakage, and malware attacks.

- *Network security*: Network infrastructure and the devices connected to it are protected through technologies, policies, and practices. Network security defends against threats such as unauthorized access and malicious use and modifications.
- *Internet security*: Internet security protects software applications, web browsers, and VPNs that use the Internet. Using techniques such as encryption and Internet security defends the transfer of data from malware attacks.

Access Control Security

Access control is a security system that directs who or what can view or use assets in a registering situation. It is essential to limit hazards to the business or association.

Access control is divided into two categories: physical and logical. Physical access limits access to grounds, structures, rooms, and physical IT resources. Intelligent access limits associations with PC systems, framework documents, and information.

One might use electronic access control frameworks to verify an office. These frameworks depend on client certifications, evaluations, and reports that follow representative access to confined business areas and exclusive territories. A typical example is a server farm. A portion of these frameworks consolidates the control boards to limit passage to rooms and structures just as a lockdown averts unapproved access or activities.

Control frameworks perform recognizable proof confirmation and approval of clients and substances by assessing required login accreditations that incorporate passwords, personal identification numbers, biometric examines, security tokens, or other verification factors. Multifaceted verification requires at least two confirmation factors and is a critical piece of layered safeguard to secure access control frameworks.

Security controls work by recognizing an individual or substance. This confirms that the individual or application is who or what it professes to be. After confirmation, the individual or application is approved for the entrance level and given access to a set of activities related with the username or IP address. Registry administrations and conventions such as Local Directory Access Protocol and the Security Assertion Markup Language are used to control and confirm, approve clients and elements, and empower them to associate with PC assets such as conveyed applications and web servers. Associations use diverse access control models that rely upon the consistency prerequisites and the dimensions of data innovation.

Intrusion Detection System

The intrusion detection system (IDS) is a custom-built system that screens traffic for suspicious activity and issues caution when suspicious movement is found. Corrective action needs to be taken when this occurs, such as blocking traffic sent from suspicious IP addresses.

IDS screens systems for possibly harmful movement; thus, they are inclined to send out false alerts. Associations need to calibrate their IDS items when they initially introduce them. The IDS should distinguish what ordinary traffic on their system looks like contrasted with possible harmful movement.

An Intrusion Prevention System (IPS) screens organization's systems for conceivably harmful system traffic. IPS frameworks react to such traffic by logging the traffic, issuing warnings, and dismissing the possibly harmful packages.

IPS

An IPS is a preventative measure used to distinguish potential dangers and react to them quickly. Similar to an IDS, an IPS screens a range of traffic and can act promptly when needed. Typically, an IPS may drop a parcel that later decides to be malicious and obstruct all further traffic from that IP address or port. The more effective approach is to send the beneficiary with no obvious disturbance or delay of administration.

Instances of Data Security

Other instances of data security need to be considered and are crucial to maintaining the integrity of data security. It is important to review the unapproved or unintentional revelation of grouped or delicate data. It is worth looking at an e-mail containing arranged or delicate data sent to wrong beneficiaries. This can lead to robbery or loss of characterized or delicate data. An example of this might be a printed version of arranged or delicate data stolen from a disposable bag or left in an environment.

Network Security

Network security requires policies and practices to protect the network of an organization (Mannes and Maziero 2019). These policies and practices help the organization protect itself from attacks such as unauthorized access, tampering of data, and denial of service attacks. Firewalls must be installed to protect systems and data. Access control lists must be created to enable the users with the required authorization to have access to data and the systems and to restrict access for others. Security groups can increase security if the organization is using Cloud-based technologies. To increase security, the organization can create VPNs to enable required resources to be shared among users based on their subnetworks. This provides an added advantage for overall productivity resources.

Physical Security

Every organization should be capable of having the best authentication scheme through building up the best access control and by installing firewalls and intrusion prevention. The organization security space can be breached despite these measures. This can happen very quickly if the organization did not take the steps to implement physical security. Physical security is the protection of the real equipment and systems that store and transmit data resources. To execute physical security, all companies must recognize the vulnerable assets and take measures to guarantee that these assets are safe from a physical security breach. Below are the measures that can be taken by organizations:

1. *Locked doors:* All doors must be locked. Employers should not allow unauthorized people to enter the building without proper identification. It is the organization's responsibility to request individuals to

identify themselves before entering the building. High-esteem data assets should be verified in an area with constrained access.

2. *Physical intrusion detection:* Every organization should place security cameras and metal detectors in buildings with high-esteemed data assets. This helps detect illegal passing into data centers.

3. *Secured equipment:* All devices ought to be secured to keep them from being stolen. One representative's hard drive could contain most of the client data, so it is essential that it be secured.

4. *Environmental monitoring:* All company servers and other high-esteem gear should be kept in a secure place that is continuously checked for appropriate temperature, moistness, and airflow. The danger of a server failure rises when these factors leave a predefined extent.

5. *Employee training:* All employers should be trained on how to lock their laptops and systems when they are away. Employees should always keep their eyes on their laptop and cellphone when traveling. This is the most widely recognized way criminals take corporate data.

Application Security

Denial of service attacks can be stopped by employing black hole routing. All the traffic related to attacks will be sent to a black hole, which is usually a nonexistent server. Some attackers will orchestrate attacks that will have signatures associated with them. These types of attacks can be best dealt with by employing an IPS. The traffic used for attacks can be from more than one source. This can be countered with upstream filtering, where cleaning centers and scrubbing centers are used.

Determine Security Mitigations

It is very important that security issues within an organization are mitigated (de Vet, Eriksen, Booth, and French 2019). This section will consist of security policies and procedures. Some guidelines will be adapted to adhere to security standards. Security management will be followed for the security challenges. This will be done using the guidelines and principles. An organization can intensify the probabilities that its information security guidelines and principles will be affected.

Security Policy and Process and Security Standards

Security policies are a set of rules and regulations that protect the organization's information and other sensitive data. These policies include guidelines on employee access to organization information. Security policies establish the role and value of each staff member in the organization, which reduces security issues. For this reason, every organization needs to enhance its security policies to keep sensitive data safe.

In most cases, the management of an organization configures details before enhancing security policies. These details include defining who has authorized access to the organization system data and who can access the information. This system reduces the number of people who can access the organization's sensitive data. The organization must limit access to the viewing and modification of the information to the authorized staff who are accountable for any destruction, viewing, or modification of the data. This approach enables the organization to hold the authorized staff accountable for their actions within the system. Through the configuration of these details, the organization can develop and enhance security policies.

Security policies can be enhanced by limiting access to sensitive data. Employees should be allowed to access only what they need. The other way of enhancing security policies is by identifying the organization's sensitive data. The data need to be secured with strong passwords after the sensitive data have been identified and access has been limited. Strong passwords include different characters, making it difficult for hackers to discover the password. The other method of preventing hackers is to change the password regularly while maintaining the strength of the passwords. The last method that the organization needs to embrace is having either manual or automatic data backup plans. This is relevant in times of cyberattacks and data breaches.

When security policies are implemented, the productivity and security of an organization increases and security issues are reduced. Employees will be expected to sign a document of acknowledgment that helps as a legal perspective.

Information Security Policy: Identify Issues

Here are some security policy issues:

- Escalation of suspicion toward the administration's assurance to the information environment.
- Diminishing the efficiency of the information safety guidelines and principles.
- Escalation of the possible expensive information safety disappointments.

Identify Policy Users

- Different programs have diverse information safety roles and everyday jobs. The organization's receptionist, lead IT director, and vendor all have different accountabilities. These different types of operators may include:
- Management, as well as panels, managerial supervision, and other administration.
- Information structure staffs, including workforces, freelancers, and counselors.

Information Security Policy: Categorization

Information security policies and standards can translate into these meaningful categories:

- Preliminary guidelines and principles, including information safety management arrangement and responsibilities.
- Guidelines and principles for workforces and other information operators.
- Organization and application enlargement guidelines and principles.

Information Security Policy: Review

Review draft policies and standards with management, users, and legal counsel. Organizations and operators will support the guidelines and principles and verify that the guidelines and principles are reliable in the industry and necessary for the business. Information safety guidelines and principles must be revised by the organization to be recognized as a lawful entity that fulfills local, state, and country laws.

Information Security Policy: Training

Train all the workforce and personnel in the organizations to adhere with the information security policies and standards. All human resources employees need to deliver their work steadily (Collins 2019). It is important to provide awareness and teach others to do the same. Without such training and education, employees will not deliver their duties with precision.

- The organization must protect risky informational properties.
- Management must provide assurance that they will safeguard risky informational properties.

Information Security Policy: Implementation

Enforce the organizations information security policies.

Implementation should be based on the guidelines and principles created to maintain the required standard. Unless guidelines and principles are consistently required, the business may find itself in lawful jeopardy. In this case, the organization must elect to implement the guidelines and principles, typically if the implementation is focused against an individual in a legally sheltered period. Technology can make it easier to enforce certain information safety guidelines and principles.

Information Security Policy

Review and modify policies and standards annually. Technology prospects will be considered in the case of business and functioning requirements, along with lawful responsibilities and duties. Information safety guidelines and principles must progress to reproduce altering environments. Safety guidelines and principles can be analyzed and transformed to comply with the new rules, regulations, standards set by government organizations and industry regulations.

Malware Protection

One way to protect the organization system from malware is itemized below (Xue, Li, Wu, Tian, and Wang 2019). IT must install approved anti-malware software on all workplaces and servers to avoid, notice, and eliminate malicious code. IT configures anti-malware software so that the following items are taken care of:

- All files coming from external sources are checked before implementation or usage.
- Suspected malware is logged, and the IT and security team are notified.
- Daily full malware scans are directed to IT and the security team.
- Malware signature files are restructured daily.
- Program alerts are installed and send information on malware incidents to respective security personnel.

Security Information Classifications

Information owners determine the sensitivity of the information belonging to them (Stafford, Deitz, and Li 2019). This determines a standard that everyone must follow to protect professional information. Information is broken into three categories:

1. Public information
2. Internal use only information
3. Restricted information

Login ID and Passwords

It is important that appropriate login and password standards are in place to help make the system secure.

Access to the organization's IT network and information systems is succeeded by access control techniques. Before gaining access to the organization's IT network systems or protected information systems, a user must present a login identification and a password. Both are unique to the user, which provides a measure of confidence that the user is who he or she claims to be.

Security policies help an organization secure its sensitive data and protect the organization's interests. Additionally, it helps the employees understand the value of the organization and the critical information that is not to be shared with people outside the organization. Finally, security policies protect an organization against information breaches.

Cybersecurity Layers

The cybersecurity layers are shown in Figure 2.1. Each of the layers are described (Bolla, Carrega, and Repetto 2019; Swire 2018).

Cybersecurity Process

Cybersecurity Process Mission Critical Approach for Organizations:

- Prevention: policy management
  a. IT security governance
  b. Security policies and compliance
  c. Cyber threats intelligence
  d. Threat modelling
  e. Security architecture and design
  f. Security management
  g. Penetration testing
  h. Continuous Certification and Accreditation (C&A)
  i. Security awareness training
  j. Vulnerability assessment

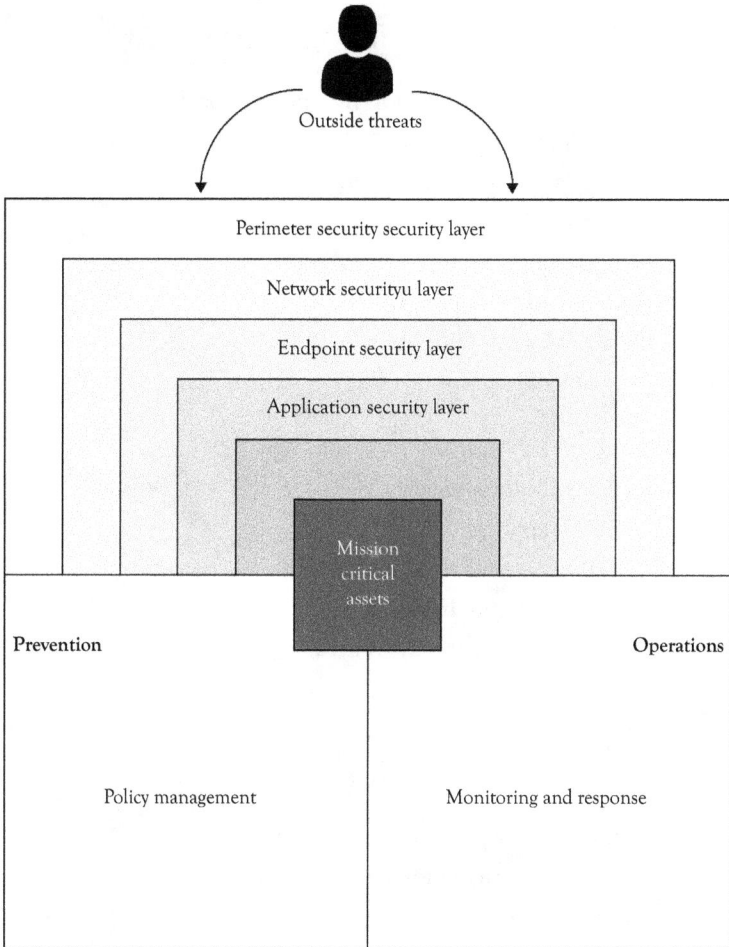

Figure 2.1 Cybersecurity layers

- Operations: monitoring and response
    a. Security operations center and network operations center monitoring (24×7)
    b. Incidence reporting, detection, and response
    c. Focus operations
    d. Continuous monitoring and assessment of situational awareness
    e. Security dashboard
    f. Escalation management
    g. Security information and event management
    h. Security level agreement (SLA) and service level object reporting

- Data security
  a. The public key infrastructure
  b. Data at rest (DAR), data in motion, and data in use (DIU)
  c. Data wiping and cleansing
  d. Identify and assess management
  e. Enterprise right management
  f. Data classification
  g. Data integrity management
  h. Data/drive encryption
  i. Data loss prevention (DLP)

- Application security
  a. Static application review
  b. Dynamic application testing
  c. Web application firewall (WAF)
  d. Database and monitoring scanning
  e. Database secure gateway (Shield)

- Endpoint security
  a. Desktop firewall
  b. Host IDS/IPS
  c. Content security (antivirus and anti-malware)
  d. Endpoint security enforcement
  e. Federal desktop core compliance
  f. Patch management
  g. DLP

- Network security perimeter security
  a. Enclave and datacenter firewall
  b. Enterprise IDS/IPS
  c. VoIP protection
  d. Inline patching
  e. Web proxy content filtering
  f. Network access control (NAC)
  g. Enterprise message security
  h. Enterprise remote access
  i. DLP

- Perimeter security
  a. Perimeter firewall
  b. Perimeter IDS/IPS
  c. Secure DMZs
  d. Message security (antivirus and anti-malware)
  e. Honeypot
  f. DLP
  g. DHS Einstein

The above listed items are described in detail below.

- Prevention: Policy Management
  a. IT Security Governance: This involves controlling IT security using the ISO 38500 standard framework. The governance specifies framework accountability and provides the necessary oversight to ensure that controls are deployed for the sole reason of mitigating risks.
  b. Security Policies and Compliance: A layout for the organization will detail a plan to protect the organization physically along with the organization's IT assets. The compliance and policy practice focuses on identifying controls for compliance regimens such as software risk, setting organizational software security policy, and auditing against that policy.
  c. Cyber Threats Intelligence: Cyber threats intelligence is one of the most critical weapons that can be used in cyber defense when it comes to identifying a possible attacker. This type of defense details how, why, and when the attackers plan to attack. The intent is to provide the organization with peace of mind and stop cyber threats.
  d. Threat Modeling: The motive behind threat modeling is to structure activities for identifying and managing threats. This strategy can be used with a wide range of activities such as applications, systems, networks, IoTs, and business processes. The rationale for threat modeling is to do the following:

1. Build a secure application.
2. Document, identify, and rate threats.
3. Find security flaws when there is time to fix them.
4. To save time, revenue, and the reputation of the organization.
5. Provide knowledge and awareness of the latest risks and vulnerabilities.

Threat modeling includes assets (data and equipment that can be secured), threats (determine what the attackers can do), and vulnerabilities (flaws that can be in the system).

Security architecture and design: to provide architectural and security design for the organization.

Security management: to provide full security management for the organization through evaluating the IT infrastructure and safely trying to exploit vulnerabilities. The improper configurations or vulnerabilities may exist in the operating systems, services, application flaws, or risky end user.

Security awareness training: This is an organizational attempt to provide security training to the workforce. The training can remain ongoing.

   o Vulnerability assessment: This is the process of defining,
      identifying, classifying, and prioritizing the vulnerabilities
      that exist in the organization computer systems, applica-
      tions, and network infrastructures. This assessment provides
      the organization with the necessary knowledge, awareness,
      and security background to understand threats.

• Operations: Monitoring and Response
   1. Security operations center and network operations center moni-
      toring (24×7): The security operations center and network oper-
      ations center's intent is to monitor the data center 24×7. The
      center requires a well-trained workforce. The workforce needs to
      maintain the network and the servers. The network operations
      center ensures that the overall network infrastructure does not
      interrupt network service. The duties include protecting the fol-
      lowing: networks, websites, applications, databases, servers and
      data centers, and other technologies.

2. Incidence reporting, detection, response: This system reports security incidents, detects possible security issues, and proactively provides appropriate responses.

3. Focus operations: A team is formed to focus on specific security concerns. The team will provide corrective actions for identifying security concerns.

4. Continuous monitoring and assessment situational awareness: This strategy routinely monitors the cyber environment for possible concerns and carries out assessments, which provides awareness.

5. Security dashboard: The security dashboard provides a one-stop overview of security visibility to the security workforce. This makes it easy to take proactive actions promptly and quickly.

6. Escalation management: Escalation management focuses on security incidents and problems. This approach lets the appropriate team handle the incident.

7. Security information and event management: This approach to security management uses security information management and security event management functions. These functions are bunched into one security management system.

8. Digital forensics: This is the recovery and investigation of material found in digital devices, often in relation to computer crime or cyberattacks. The technical aspect of the investigation is usually divided into several sub-branches that relate to the type of digital devices involved. These devices include computer forensics, network forensics, forensic data analysis, and mobile device forensics. The forensic process covers the seizure, forensic acquisition, and analysis of digital media and products that collect evidence.

9. SLA and service level object reporting: An SLA is an agreement that the organization provides the customers for the services available. The service level object is where the service wants to reach. The SLA is the operation level agreement and an agreement between the internal support groups of the organization.

- Data Security
  1. Public key infrastructure: The public key infrastructure is a set of roles, policies, and procedures required to create, manage, distribute, use, store and revoke digital certificates, and manage public key encryption. The framework of encryption and cybersecurity protects communications between the server organization website and the client. This uses two different cryptographic keys: a public key and a private key.
  2. DAR, data in motion, and DIU: The DAR, data in motion, and DIU are used to protect data in the organization. The smart way to protect DAR is to encrypt the data before it is written into the storage system. The data cannot be accessed without the encryption key and algorithm. DIU blocks access from one application memory space into another to avoid data leaks or corruption. Modern hardware provides physical layers of support and modern operating systems to keep each application in its own "sandbox." This allows individuals to access the resources the individual is authorized to access, warranting it safe. Data sent to the external system may have security constraints. This makes DIU safer. It is recommended that data for implementation are protected with encrypted channels on both ends of the systems to protect from remote access via the VPN.
  3. Data wiping and cleansing: This software-based method can be adapted to clean data that are aimed at destroying the hard disk or data that are available on digital media devices. This method is often referred to as data clearing or data wiping.
  4. Identify and assess management: The identification and assess management approach combines policy data loss with information rights management to avoid the loss of sensitive data. The sensitive data are defined as data with a sensitive keyword or phrase.
  5. Enterprise right management: This is part of digital rights management. This technology can protect possible information from being stolen.
  6. Data classification: Data classification is based on groups with common characteristics. These categories help protect data more

effectively. Classified data makes the data easier to locate and retrieve. Data classification is important when it comes to security management, compliance, and data security. The organization leadership need to be involved in data classification.

7. Data integrity management: Data integrity management encapsulates the consistency and accuracy maintenance of data. This maintenance includes critical design and implementation usage of the system the data are stored on. It is important to maintain data because organizations depend on the accuracy of the data to make decisions. Data integrity management can be accomplished by completing the following:

   a. Introduce the data.
   b. Perform risk-based validation on the data.
   c. Select appropriate system and service providers outside the organization when necessary.
   d. Audit the organization's audit trails.
   e. Change control must be in place.
   f. Quality IT and validation systems should be implemented in the organization.
   g. Plan for business continuity.
   h. Treat and maintain data with accuracy.

8. Data and drive encryption: This aims at making data unintelligible to anyone who is not authorized to use the data. Usually, this is the requirement of the organization compliance that must be met by all users. McAfee drive encryption can be used for this.

9. DLP: This is a software that scans information after the firewall phase. Security policies are applied to the data and determine if the data contain a certain keyword or phrase that may lead to a security attack.

- Application Security
   1. Static application review: This is a set of technologies for analyzing application source, binary, and byte codes to identify application vulnerabilities. This analysis is carried out when the

application is not running. The process helps clarify the code structure and helps organizations adhere to the industry standard.

2. Dynamic application testing: This is a program that identifies potential security vulnerabilities by communicating through the web front-end. Black box tests are carried out and help identify security vulnerabilities by performing attacks through minimal user interactions via hostname, authentication credentials, query strings, headers, and fragments. The customer will benefit knowing that the application environment is safe.

3. WAF: WAF is used for HTTP applications that use a set of rules to communicate within HTTP. The communications are geared toward attacks such as cross-site scripting and sequel injection. WAF protects servers and usually comes in the form of an appliance, server plugin, or filter. WAF is usually customizable based on an organization's settings.

4. Database and monitoring scanning: This scanning carries out database monitoring that consists of security auditing and real-time security monitoring and analyzing. This process is done independently. This scanning provides protection to sensitive database from external cyberattacks. Most data breaches tend to come from compromised data servers.

5. Database secure gateway (Shield): Rampant use of the Internet and databases lead to a possibility of experiencing threats. This ought to be protected. The sequel attack has woken users to other possible attacks. The security gateway between the web server and database server tends to solve these breaches. The shield has been used in organizations as an effective solution. One application of shield is called Firebird, which stores configuration settings and most data.

- Endpoint Security
  1. Desktop firewall: The remote firewall has successfully been used to gain administrative access to a Windows server. Windows operating system can connect remotely. A remote firewall is possible with operating systems such as Linux. Depending on the

user privileges, Linux can establish a connection to delete, read, or write files, change file permissions or settings, and configure the server. This provides an advantage to connect users who need to connect remotely.

2. Host IDS and IPS: The IDS and IPS improve the security level of an organization's network by monitoring traffic and scanning packages for possible data breaches. The IPS resides between the firewalls to stop suspected traffic from penetrating the network. The IPS monitors inbound packets, carries out analysis to determine the purpose, and may decide whether it is appropriate to allow the packet into the network. This is powerful and healthy to the network and the server.

3. Content security (antivirus and anti-malware): This is a computer security standard used to prevent IT cross-site scripting, clickjacking, and other means of web page context website injection attacks. The organization decides which of the following can be used: JavaScript, CSS, HTML frames, web workers, fonts, images, embeddable objects such as Java applets, ActiveX, audio and video files, and other HTML5 features.

4. Endpoint security enforcement: This is a policy standard enforced by organizations. The endpoint is an Internet-capable computer hardware device on a transmission control protocol/Internet protocol (TCP/IP) network that applies to desktop computers, laptops, smartphones, tablets, thin clients, printers, or other specialized hardware. The purpose of the endpoint policy is to protect the endpoints from vulnerable security attacks on the infrastructure or customer data.

5. Federal desktop core compliance: Federal desktop core compliance is a recommended list for a general purpose microcomputers that have a connection to other networks. The purpose is to provide more secure and reliable security measures with the federal government. The federal government demands that these standards are met. This mandatory standard came to effect on February 1, 2008. The following guidelines are mandated by the federal government (Information Technology: Federal Laws,

Regulations, and Mandatory Standards for Securing Private Sector Information Technology Systems and Data in Critical Infrastructure Sectors, 2008).

o Federal desktop core compliance demands that only to Windows XP and Vista desktop and laptop computers are replaced by the United States Government Configuration Baseline that includes settings for Windows 7 and Red Hat Enterprise Linux 5.

o For Windows 7, the National Institute of Standards and Technology (NIST) demands the naming convention to the U.S. Government Computer Baseline, or USGCB version 2.0. This led to an un-classified general Windows settings guide. The NIST published the guides specifically for Windows Firewall and Internet Explorer. A guide (Vista-Energy, for example) was created to capture settings that adhere to energy conservation policies.

6. Patch management: This process helps acquire test and install multiple patches (changes to application software) on existing applications. This enables the existing application or hardware system software to stay current. Life cycle policies acquire, test, and install multiple patches of software or existing application.

7. DLP: DLP is used to prevent information leakage. During the incident, the DLP is used to help summarize what is going on within seven days. Once the problem of leakage is diagnosed, the organization can focus on a specific solution that will prevent data loss.

- Network security and perimeter security
  1. Enclave and datacenter firewall: This is a Windows Server 2016 tool. It is a network layer with the following features: 5-tuple (protocol, source, and destination port numbers along with source and destination IP addresses), state-full, and multitenant firewall. The administrator can install and configure policies to help protect virtual network traffic from unwanted traffic on the intranet network and Internet.

2. Enterprise IDS and IPS: The IDS and IPS improve the security level of an organization's network by monitoring traffic and scanning packages for possible data breaches. The IPS resides between the firewalls to stop suspected traffic from penetrating the network. The IPS monitors inbound packets, carries out analysis to determine the purpose, and may decide whether it is appropriate to allow the packet into the network. This is powerful and healthy to the network and the server.

3. VoIP Protection: VoIP is a new type of Internet application that carries out real-time data streaming using the IP address (a unique string of numbers separated by periods that identifies each computer using the Internet protocol to communicate over a network). The security used to protect text, applications, FTP to Web, e-mail, and instant messaging can be used to improve VoIP security. Here are recommendations for protecting the VoIP:

   o Ensure the current patch for the operating system and VoIP applications.
   o Only use applications required to provide and maintain VoIP services.
   o Mandate strong authentication for administrative and user account access.
   o Require maintenance for user accounts and have standards that will deter hackers from breaking into the operating system.
   o Enforce stringent authorization policies to avoid hackers' access to VoIP service and account data.
   o Enforce administrative audits and user sessions and frequently complete service-related activities.
   o Enforce policy and implementation standards for installs to maintain server firewalls, anti-malware, and anti-tampering measures to deter *denial-of-service* (DoS) attacks.
   o Enforce stringent security implementation to secure VoIP applications and prevent misuse. Typically, a whitelist of callable country codes is used to thwart certain calls,

transfers, and social engineering exploits that might result in toll fraud and unauthorized use.

4. Inline patching: This is an advanced method that checks the integrity of protected code when patching an application in a system. If application changes are detected, the file update will be stopped without any prompt. This serves as a security precaution to any patch that needs to be carried out. When protection file starts immediately, threads are established and may be executed manually. These threats are periodically checked for integrity against the protected code. The delay between the checkups of each thread is defined in the inline checkup delay field for accuracy or matching numbers. The optimal value for the protection thread should be three to five; however, the number can go to 15. High numbers translate to a high Central Processing Unit loading. The threads can be selected after complete testing of the protected file. The checkup of each protected thread is measured in milliseconds. This checkup should be done after the first test on the protected file and then the optimal value can be selected.

5. Web proxy content filtering: Web proxy content filtering is a network security system to protect network resources at the application layer. A proxy firewall acts as an intermediary between in-house clients and Internet servers. The proxy server has the capacity to provide security depending on the organization use case, needs, or policy.

6. Network access control: This approach to computer security makes every effort to unify endpoints technology, such as host intrusion protection, antivirus, and vulnerability assessments that include use and system authentication and network security enforcement.

7. Enterprise message security: This enterprise mobile messaging stage caters to the requirements of the organization. It offers key features such as advanced security, administrative access, message reliability, and integrated mobile application that provide a user-friendly experience for the consumer third-party messaging application. This system meets the required standard of

the Financial Industry Regulatory Authority, HIPPA, and Sarbanes-Oxley.

8. Enterprise remote access: This approach connects organization's networks remotely. The connection to the organization's server requires ongoing remote support, which may come with significant risks if not managed properly. SecureLink can provide the required security needs. SecureLink can provide the following benefits:

   o Eliminate security issues that come with shared logins with ad hoc supporting needs.

   o Provide remote access with a simple interface.

   o Stay in compliance with required rules and regulations of the organization.

   o Keep the organization vendors accountable for their actions.

9. DLP: DLP is used to prevent information leakage. During the incident, the DLP is used to summarize what is going on within seven days. Once the problem of leakage is diagnosed, the organization can focus on a specific solution that will prevent data loss.

- Perimeter Security

   1. Perimeter firewall: This is related to DMZs, which are physical or logical subnetworks that contain and expose the organization's external-facing services to the unfriendly or classified untrusted network. A good method for perimeter security is to protect the application's data and services.

   2. Perimeter IDS and IPS: IDS and IPS are family security solutions that try and locate anomalous traffic on the network.

   3. Secure DMZs: The secure DMZ serves as a buffer zone between the public Internet and the organizational network. It deploys DMZ between two firewalls by screening all inbound packages for a firewall or other security appliances before the package reaches the server end of the organization.

   4. Message security (antivirus and anti-malware): Message security protects data and messages from unauthorized access. Data secu-

rity includes encryption, tokenization, and key management practices with in-depth protection of both the data and the messages. Organizations should regularly backups files (backup copies should be stored in fireproof safes or in another building) and run antivirus software.

5. Honeypot: Honeypot is an approach that lures attackers into the computer system. The intention is to mimic targets of cyberattacks. This approach is used to detect attacks, deflect the attacks, and to keep cybercriminals out while nonattackers keep using the system harmoniously. The attackers believe the honeypot is a legitimate target, but when they come for it, it turns out to be a bait. This allows the system administrator to monitor system traffic to better understand where cybercriminals are coming from, how they operate, and what they want. This method can also determine which security measures to use and which ones to improve upon.

6. DLP: DLP is used to prevent information leakage. During the incident, the DLP is used to help summarize what is going on within seven days. Once the problem of leakage is diagnosed, the organization can focus on a specific solution that will prevent data loss.

7. DHS Einstein: DHS Einstein is an IDS designed to monitor and analyze Internet traffic as it moves in and out of the U.S. government networks. This system identifies patterns of attacks and prompts a notification to the US-CERT and several Government agencies. It has been reported that DHS Einstein fails to detect 94 percent of threats and does not monitor web traffic, which is the main purpose.

Cybersecurity falls into the following categories: physical, data link, network, transportation, session, presentation, and application.

Physical: This is the lowest layer where hardware shares the same physical, real-world space as the user. Locks are put on doors to keep systems safe.

Data link: At this layer, the data are just one level above the bare metal and silicon of the hardware. The data move from software to hardware and back. Security at this layer keeps the traffic going and the data where it is supposed to be.

Network: This consists of traffic control with speed limits, detours, and stop signs. This is where the network addressing, routing, and other traffic controls take place. Security at this layer protects against flooding attacks and snooping or sniffing attacks to keep criminals from accessing logins and passwords sent over the network.

Transportation: This is the post office; it gets mail from point A to point B reliably and without anyone tampering with the contents. This layer deals with data, computers, and networks. Denial-of-service attacks also occur here, as well as man-in-the-middle attacks that intercept the data between point A and point B.

Session: The session is a continuous exchange of information in the form of multiple back-and-forth transmissions. The session layer controls the connections between computers. A typical example is denial-of-service and spoofing.

Presentation: The presentation layer is below the application layer and transforms data into the form that the application accepts. Typically, it feeds the HTML code to a web browser and produces a webpage. It can be given to the phone texting application.

Application: The application layer is closest to the end user and is most affected by cyber attackers. Typically, web browsers and e-mail clients are attacked at this layer. Attackers interact with computers and devices.

Security Management Process

There are three primary areas that security controls fall under. These areas are management security, operational security, and physical security controls:

- *Management security* is the overall design of your controls. Management security provides guidance, rules, and procedures for implementing a secure environment.
- *Operational security* is the effectiveness of your controls. This includes access control, authentication, and security topologies after network installations are complete.

- *Physical security* is the protection of personnel, data, and hardware from physical threats that could harm, damage, or disrupt business operations or impact the confidentiality, integrity, or availability of systems and data.

Information security provides strong foundations for risk management decisions. It is appropriate to design security assessments to arm the organization with the information needed to fully understand the risks and compliance obligations.

System software: This is a generic term for an organized collection of computer data and instructions. The two types of software are application software and system software. Application software helps users solve a problem or carry out a specific task. A word processor is an example of application software.

System software coordinates the functions of hardware and software and controls the operations of computer hardware. A computer's operating system is an example of system software. Operating systems control the computer hardware and act as an interface with application programs. The system software also includes utility software, device drivers, and firmware.

Utility software: Utility software helps manage, maintain, and control computer resources. Operating systems typically contain the necessary tools for this, but separate utility programs can provide improved functionality. Utility software is somewhat technical and targets users with a solid knowledge of computers. You may not have much need for these utilities if you only use a computer for e-mail, some Internet browsing, and typing; however, if you are an avid computer user, these utilities can help make sure your computer has a defense against cybersecurity issues. Examples of utility programs are antivirus software, backup software, and disk tools.

Antivirus software: As the name suggests, antivirus software helps protect a computer system from viruses and other harmful programs. A computer virus is a computer program that can cause damage to a computer's software, hardware, or data. It is referred to as a virus because it can replicate itself and hide inside other computer files.

One of the most common ways to get a virus is to download a file from the Internet. Antivirus software scans your online activity to make sure you are not downloading infected files. New viruses come out all the time, so antivirus software needs to be updated very frequently.

Backup software: This helps in the creation of backup files on the computer. Most computer systems use a hard disk drive for storage. While these are generally very robust, these disk drives can fail or crash, resulting in costly data loss. Backup software helps you copy the most important files to another storage device such as an external hard disk. You can also make an exact copy of your hard disk.

Increasingly, backup software uses Cloud storage to create backups. This typically means you pay a fee to use the storage space of a third party and use their backup software to manage which files are going to be backed up.

A range of disk tools can help manage hard disk drives and other storage devices. This includes utilities that scan the hard disks for any potential problems, disk cleaners to remove any unnecessary files, and disk defragmenters to reorganize file fragments and increase performance. Disk tools are important because the failure of a hard disk drive can have disastrous consequences. Keeping disks running efficiently is an important part of overall computer maintenance.

Operation Security Process

Identify Critical Information

An organization can classify critical information based on the organization's standards. Typical critical data will fall under the categories of military, political, strategic, monetary, and mechanical data. An organization's business can be harmed when this set of data is compromised.

Threat Assessment

Operations security defensive measures must be created. The threat evaluation project in the operations security procedure distinguishes potential enemies and their related abilities and constraints, and aims to gather, break down, and use the compromised information against the organization. The threat alludes to more than an adversary specialist taking cover behind a stone.

Vulnerability Analysis

Operational or mission-related powerlessness exists when the enemy can gather markers, accurately investigate them, and make an opportune move. The weakness of the system makes the environment vulnerable. Compromised information can be uncovered through gathered and broke down markers, which creates vulnerabilities. Data need to be protected but remain friendly.

Security Assessment

Operations security officers work with different organizers and give hazard appraisals and prescribe activities to moderate vulnerabilities. At that point, commandants determine whether to use the operations security measures. Hazard evaluations measure an adversary's capacity to abuse defenselessness and the potential harm on the activities. The evaluations also give money-saving tips of possible techniques to control the accessibility of compromised information.

Measures and Countermeasures

Activity security measures and countermeasures protect organizations by anticipating hostile misuse of compromised information. Countermeasures moderate or evacuate vulnerabilities that uncover compromised information. These countermeasures deal with crude information, upgrade neighborly power capacities by expanding the potential for shock, and increase the viability of well-disposed information systems.

Determine Security Mitigation

The steps below detail ways to curb or reduce security issues; however, a thorough check must be conducted using some form of mitigation approach to make sure the environment is well secured.

Step #1: Identify and Document Asset Vulnerabilities

The first step should be a security assessment to understand what makes the organization attractive to cybercriminals (customer data is likely to be the biggest commodity at risk) and where the main vulnerabilities lie.

A good starting point is to ask some basic questions, such as "What information does the organization collect?" "How does the organization store information?" and "Who has access to the information?" Next, one should examine how the data are currently being protected and how the organization's computers, network, e-mail, and other tools are secured.

For example, consider whether the organization has a formal written policy for social media usage on any device (including employees' devices) that connects to the organization network. Does the organization provide Internet safety training for the workforce? Does the organization wipe all old machines of data before disposal? Does the organization require multifactor authentication (more than one way of confirming a user's claimed identity) to access the network?

Step #2: Identify and Document Internal and External Threats

Organizations should be familiar with the main types of crime and how they are perpetrated. This includes the tactics, techniques, and procedures used to target organizations. The organization's workforce should not focus exclusively outwards but consider looking inside the organization, too. While the word "hacker" may be perceived as a teenager in a bedroom in some remote corner of the world, it may not always be the case.

Step #3: Assess Your Vulnerabilities

Many free tools are available for computer scanning; however, an organization should be prepared to invest in such tools and services. Organizations should determine what services are running to determine whether the software version is up to date and expose known vulnerabilities. Some tools allow the IT administrator to run predefined exploits against the organization's systems and use brute-force attacks against its own end users. The workforce may wish to go one step further and appoint an outside security specialist to gauge the organization's resilience through penetration testing, similar to the way vehicle manufacturers use tame burglars to break into cars.

Step #4: Identify Potential Business Impacts and Likelihoods

A business impact analysis determines the effects or consequences—including financial, operational, and reputational—of an attack on the organization business. The organization's continuity or resilience plan should already have a clear picture of the costs linked to IT failures or business interruption. If not, a specialist can guide the organization through this process, and ready-to-use questionnaires are available to help collect information from various parts of the organization's continuity or resilience plan. Step #5: Identify and Prioritize the Security Responses

A good starting point for the IT workforce is to prioritize how the organization will resolve any immediate security flaws. Any security system changes should be tested to ensure all holes are closed and verify that the changes have not negatively impacted any other systems. The organization should retest security liability to ensure rules and best practices are documented in policies. It is important to undertake a continuous education to educate staff on the risks that come from today's interconnected ways of doing business (*5 Steps to Assess and Mitigate Cybersecurity Risks*, n.d.).

Operational Standards

A security standard is like any other standard in any other industry. A standard is a published specification that establishes a common language and contains a technical specification or other precise criteria. Standards are designed to be used consistently as a rule, a guideline, or a definition.

Information security management standards are primarily concerned with ensuring the existence of processes rather than the content of these processes. A process refers to a set of principles by which systems are rendered secure. For example, "carry out a security analysis" and "set up an awareness program" are examples of principles that are part of the process. This lack of attention to the content problem manifests itself in two ways. First, it means the standards are more concerned with ensuring certain information security activities exist in organizations and are less interested in how well they are done. Second, the processes, guidelines, and principles provided by the information security management standards are abstract and simplified and do not provide advice on how the desired results are to be achieved in practice.

The goal of security standards is to improve the security of IT systems, networks, and critical infrastructures. A security standard defines both functional and assurance requirements in a product, system, process, or technology environment. Well-developed security standards enable consistency among product developers and serve as a reliable metric for purchasing security products. Security standards cover a broad range of granularity, from the mathematical definition of a cryptographic algorithm to the specification of security features in a web browser. These features are typically implementation independent. A standard must address user needs but must also be practical since cost and technological limitations must be considered. Additionally, a standards requirement must be verifiable; otherwise, users cannot assess security even when products are tested against the standard.

Some of the examples are as follows:

Cybersecurity standards are proliferating. Governments and businesses increasingly mandate their implementation. More manufacturers and vendors are building and selling standards-compliant products and services and a growing number of organizations are becoming involved in standards development. Cybersecurity standards are being embraced because they are useful. They provide tangible benefits that justify the time and financial resources required to produce and apply them.

The Payment Card Industry Data Security Standard (PCI DSS) was developed to encourage and enhance cardholder data security and facilitate the broad adoption of consistent data security measures globally. PCI DSS provides a baseline of technical and operational requirements designed to protect account data. PCI DSS applies to all entities involved in payment card processing, including merchants, processors, acquirers, issuers, and service providers. PCI DSS also applies to all other entities that store, process, or transmit cardholder data and sensitive authentication data.

Security Standards

The different organizational security standards are as follows:

An existing process is used for maintaining the security of assets when creating policies for an established organization. These policies are used as drivers for the policies. Standards can be coined to establish the analysts' mandatory mechanisms for implementing the policy when there are no technology drivers.

Standards help create a successful environment despite the organization's difficult policies. If the access policy requires one-time-use passwords, the standard for using a token device can make interoperability a relative certainty.

Information is an organization's most important asset and exposes organizations to threats that intend to explore their vulnerabilities and cause considerable damage. Policies regarding information systems security such as ISO/IEC 27002–2005 must be implemented to reduce the chances of fraud or information loss. It is important to find the security policy's critical success factors and to assess the level of importance of each one of them. This paper contributes to the identification of such factors by presenting the results of a survey regarding information systems security policies in small- and medium-sized enterprises. The discussion is in the form of a literature framework and identifies future works aiming to enhance information security in organizations.

It is well understood that security is crucial and must be included in everything an organization does. A simple look at the news provides details on the data breach of the day tied to an application security vulnerability (Watts 2017). Take a stroll to the information security department and you will hear about the latest blunder an employee made that resulted in lost data. Security is widespread and mainstream, but security culture has not kept pace with the threat landscape. Information security policies control employees' behavior and secure the use of hardware and software.

Organizations benefit from implementing information security policies to help classify their information assets and define the importance of the organization's information assets. Information security policies include several principles, regulations, methodologies, procedures, and tools created to secure the organization from threats. Employees' compliance with information security policies has become an important socio-organizational resource. Information security policies provide the employees with guidelines to guarantee information security.

It is important for organizations to have frequent training programs and educational awareness to attain the required result from the implementation of an information security policy. Security experts emphasize the importance of security awareness programs and how they can improve information security. Implementing security awareness in organizations is a challenging process as it requires actively building a healthy security culture.

An organization's security culture requires care and nurturing. The workforce must put in constant effort. A sustainable security culture is bigger than just a single event. When a security culture is sustainable, it transforms security from a one-time event into a life cycle that generates security returns for the organization.

Sustainable security culture can be separated into four parts. First and foremost, sustainable security is deliberate and disruptive. The primary goal of a security culture is to make a change and create better security, so it must be disruptive to the organization and deliberate with a set of actions to foster the change. Second, it must be engaging and fun to implement. The workforce should enjoy the security culture while being challenged. Third, it is rewarding for the workforce and worth investing time and effort into. Fourth, it provides a return on investment. The rationale is to improve the offering and lower vulnerabilities.

A strong security culture will consist of interactions in day-to-day procedures but also defines how security influences the things that your organization provides to others. Those offerings may be products, services, or solutions, but they must have security applied to all parts and pieces. A sustainable security culture is persistent; it is not a once-a-year event, but is embedded into everything the organization does.

Those involved in organization security culture believe that it is necessary. Security culture is primarily for humans, not for computers. The computer does exactly what it is directed to do. The challenge is with the humans; they will do what they think is appropriate. Humans need a framework to make appropriate security decisions. In general, employees in the organization need to do the right thing based on the organization's rules and regulations.

How organizational security has benefits: Wherever an organization sits on the security culture spectrum, changes can be made to make the culture better.

Addressing threats: Threats are everywhere, especially when it comes to IT Security and the explosion of ransomware. The goal behind IT security policies and procedures is to address those threats, implement strategies on how to mitigate those threats, and learn how to recover from threats that have exposed a portion of your organization.

The organization engages employees: Employees in the organization often have questions on culture such as: Where did these come from? Who created them? Why it being done? These are all valid questions and can be avoided when the employees are involved in the process of developing and implementing IT security policies and procedures. For obvious reasons, organizations must occasionally create and implement policies and procedures without engaging employees; however, think about the message the organization is sending when allowing employees to participate in the development or review of policies and procedures.

How management of an organization can enhance security and implementation examples are shown below.

Security policy compliance training: Our organization is obliged by law to have an information security compliance policy that provides a range of steps and measures to be followed and adhered to. Regulators reserve the right to prosecute if these policies are not in place. Compliance is not just about having a policy in place; it needs to be a living, breathing part of the organization, and the most direct approach is through providing formal compliance training. Training needs to be provided at all staff levels and should be updated regularly to take new risks or new responses into account.

Access prevention: It is necessary to constantly focus on the organization's security measures to prevent unauthorized access to sensitive data. This could range from updating the level of encryption to improving the storage security of administrative passwords. Access allowance and rules should be made clear to the whole workforce as part of the regular information security compliance training programs.

Do regular audit reports: The threats to security are continuously changing and evolving. This means the organization must regulate audit reports to assess the robustness of information security. Additionally, take measures to keep security up to date. It is important that all implementations be measured. Having regular audits allows for security improvement.

Response and remediation plan: This is a plan for when a security breach takes place rather than being taken by surprise. This approach enables the organization to be on guard. It is crucial that the organization responds to a breach timely. This shows how the organization is serious about data security and protecting the reputation of the organization.

Physical Security System and Management

Physical security can be defined as the protection of assets. This includes hardware, software, networks personnel, and data. The listed assets lead to serious damage or loss of an organization. The damages or loss could include protections that stem from a flood, fire, natural disasters (earthquakes, tornados, extreme temperatures, high humidity, heavy rains, and lightning), burglary, vandalism, theft, arson, and terrorism.

It is not every organization that pays attention to how physical security can create havoc for them. Often, the security damages are overlooked; however, when the proper approach is taken, these damages can be overcome or mitigated. Physical security can be carried out with little or no technical knowledge on the part of the attacker.

Let us look at physical security from a strategic point of view. See Figure 2.2: Typical physical security system has three component that is access control, surveillance, and testing. The following should be done to protect and make it difficult to attack physical security:

1. Ensure obstacles are placed in the way of the potential attacker. The physical sites need to be hardened to avoid accidents, attacks, and environmental disaster. The hardening can include locks, fencing, access control cards, fire suppression, and biometric access systems.
2. Care should be taken with physical locations. This may include surveillance cameras and smoke detectors.
3. Strong disaster recovery procedures and policies should be in place and tested for safety. These procedures reduce the time needed to recover from a man-made or natural disaster.

It is important to bear in mind that the IoT is growing very quickly; this needs to be taken into consideration when it comes to physical security. It is now possible for smart devices to be connected to organization systems through the Internet. This is outside the physical location of the organization; however, the organization has a responsibility to protect the organization's building. The fact that smart devices can still connect to other devices inside the physical location can pose security issues. The organization must protect the devices within the physical building. Tamper-resistant ID tags may be adequate in deterring security attackers. A possible mitigation strategy is to use higher or mission critical security devices.

After thorough identification of the security risk, it comes down to providing appropriate training to the security officers who are assigned to specifics posts. Each post will require specific training, bearing in mind that each post requires duties or post orders and procedures that will be reviewed by upper management in the organization. Subsequently, the procedures need to be reviewed periodically (e.g., every six months). The periodical review may be necessary because of the analysis of the duties and security observations. The procedures should be transparent and accessible through soft copy or hard copy. It is mandatory that the post orders should contain the following entities:

1. Revision date
2. Related confidentiality
3. Directions on dealing with public relations
4. Code of ethics related to security administrations

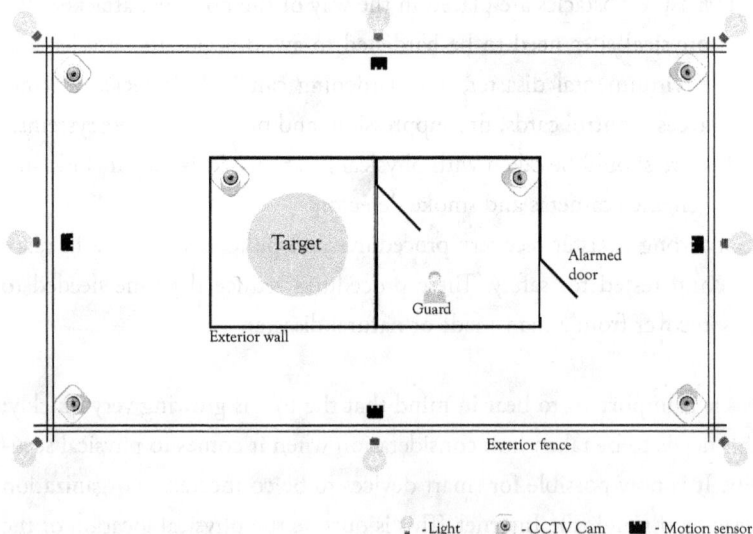

Figure 2.2 *Typical physical security system*

5. Other professional requirements that ensure security duties are done correctly

It is very helpful to use closed-circuit television to record images of people in the physical vicinity of the organization building. The video can be used as evidence in a court. It is important that the security officers keep their eyes on the television monitor and it helps to have a procedure on the length of time the security officers watch the monitor. Additionally, it helps for the security officers to be given periodic breaks. It is important that the command center operator upholds the safety of the staff members and the public, and prevents any crime. Usually, the command center operator will be watching up to 15 monitors, which requires attention to detail. The command center operator has a specific obligation to report any security issues observed or suspected quickly to other security officers before actual criminal operations take place.

It is important to bear in mind that physical security should protect the organization's employees for the simple reason that the employees are important assets to the organization. It is notable that intrusion, a detector system, firewalls, cryptography, and other security measures tend to be useless if an attacker breaks in to steal important data and assets.

CHAPTER 3

How AI and Security come together?

1. Refer to AI
2. Refer to Security
3. How AI Will Be Used in the Security?
4. Show the Learning Objectives
5. Show Examples Related to AI and Security Use Cases Together.

Chapter Outline
- How AI security come together?
- Precautions that need to be taken to protect AI system

Key Learning Points
- How AI will be used in the security?
- Show the learning objectives
- Show examples related to AI security use cases together.

How Can AI be Used for Security?

Refer to previous chapters on artificial intelligence (AI) and security for more details.

How does AI and Security come together to play a major role in the industry?

AI Security

AI uses a modernized approach to security use cases (Wells 2019). This brings a unique approach to finding security solutions. Using AI as a tool

and technique to the security use cases can be useful in solving and automating security issues. Here are some benefits:

- Saving time and money, and subsequently enabling automation of security AI.
- Able to access hidden data from a network location that is
  easily searchable.
- AI will initiate an automatic search through a massive amount
  of data to create thousands of signals. These signals give
  the security workforce insight into high confidence
  security stories that require attention to protect
  government organizations, countries, and enterprise
  organizations.
- AI automation will buy time for the security workforce
  to investigate security threats, which can be useful for the
  organization. Usually, organizations must frequently deal with
  a large amount of data; however, large amounts of data and
  archaic processes create security gaps that are predicated by
  attackers' enhanced technology.
- Devices such as Internet of things (IoT) devices, and sensors
  connecting through Wi-Fi, network, web service calls, application programming interface access, public network, and
  social media bring many possible security breaches. It is overwhelming to keep track of security issues and breaches that
  may occur in these interactions; this is the rationale behind
  using machine learning (ML).

AI Security Use Case

AI tends to have advanced technology parts that are capable of sensing,
comprehending, acting, and learning.

The current exposure to AI is impacting how businesses are running
and competing. AI provides insights that have not been thought of before,
and allows business to thrive in ways that have not been seen since the
Industrial Revolution period of the 18th century.

AI can track all the security requirements with workforce visibility. This saves time and effort. Blind spots in searching is not a weak functionality of AI.

AI can help leaders develop or implement drives to reveal new values.

AI will help leaders drive innovations to unlock trapped value in core businesses and beyond.

What could your organization achieve if every interaction with technology were intelligent?

Here are the two use cases on-premises security information and predictive cases.

The first use case is an assumption that attacks on the Cloud link security operations creates tools with the capability of providing responses and defenses based on AI reasoning. AI tools can make accurate predictions based on human behavior patterns. This could be a threat to the organization.

The second case is to protect user access. Improving the efficacy of cybersecurity will help detect and prevent cyberattacks.

Intelligently Secure Conditional Access

AI applications tend to lack the reasoning behind decisions (Gonzales Rivera, Chen, and Dahanayake 2008). These decisions are just black boxes. This is a reason why AI will not replace human workers. AI is believed to complement and support human beings. Many use cases can be cited, including speeding up routine tasks. Other use cases include detecting unusual activities or self-driving vehicles. The self-driving vehicle is currently being tested to avoid accidents and soothe human fears. Routine tasks are done accurately with defined decision rules.

Where AI Is Going

AI and human security are used to provide security protection in the physical environment of organizations. The security plan should include protection of equipment, resources, and other assets in production or office environments, including Cloud environment assets.

Physical security should consider the following: access from intruders, internal threats, cyberattacks, accidents, and natural disasters. The listed items should have a mix of technology and in-person monitoring of human security workforce. The security perimeter requires preventive measures and countermeasures.

It is helpful to consider the workforce as part of physical security for the simple reason that employees are important assets to the organization. A human can detect unseen use cases, and AI cannot. In the case of overwhelming and frequent attacks AI does a better of detecting use cases. Intrusion protection, a detector system, firewalls, cryptography, and strong data protection are strongly recommended as part of physical security.

AI and Security Marriage

It has been argued that human security teams will not be replaced soon (Fang, Qi, and Wang 2019). This may be due to trust or the fight against change. Cisco reports that cyberattacks are relentless, intelligent, and expensive. This calls for immediate action. Cyberattacks are automated and sophisticated. This creates more work for organizations and organizations must do something about this quickly. Incidents of AI malware going after defensive AI have been documented. This is a problem to watch out for. The solutions that would be ideal in this situation would be for ML and AI to fight the automated attacks. It will be helpful for ML to identify the attack's essential detection content. The attacks consist of malware and botnets that replicate and change rapidly. Predictions tell us that attackers generate a massive amount of iterations on malware every minute.

This means malware threats are exponentially increasing daily. ML and AI are tools that can handle these attacks and no human needs to be involved. ML and AI usage can be extended to incident detection and identifying risks.

Organizations should start or continue investing in a workforce that includes expertise in ML and AI and use contingency plans outside of vendors where necessary. This approach will upskill the requirements for an experienced workforce.

Advancing technology to the next level means including blockchain: the evolution from ML to true AI. Top organizations—such as the banks—are already looking at quantum computing.

Not an Overnight Transformation

AI does not transform overnight. AI can sift through many datasets, enabling it to learn from known and unknown security threats. This leads to improved security responses and solutions for security threats. Smart and autonomous security systems are necessary.

It is a fact that AI is powerful; however, AI does not make humans redundant when it comes to addressing security issues. People are still required to defend security attacks and corrective actions need to be carried out by a human. AI will continue to detect threats, defend systems, respond quickly to security events, better analyze data, and predict behaviors using statistical models. Humans struggle with pure and raw data analysis and predictions.

Use Cases for Start-Ups

Trending start-up companies are embracing AI as a security solution. Similarly, technology giants such as Google, Amazon, IBM, and Microsoft are also playing with AI security. These companies use AI to create encryption and to launch cybersecurity products in the Cloud. It is predicted that AI will soon automate a 24×7 security surveillance, which will enable organizations to concentrate on their business continuity and most critical support tasks.

AI promises to be a key weapon in cyberwarfare, but human security teams won't be replaced anytime soon (Delaney 2018).

AI can fight security attacks if it can withstand the hype. ML for malware will work well if it has the capability to generate different looks. As a result, Google has a type of ML called deep learning that has an algorithm capable of independently adjusting and self-regulating to train and evolve for the purposes of determining an attack's potential. Too much data is a problem for humanity; yet, ML learns and trains more effectively the more data it has. ML can prevent violent images, scan comments, prevent phishing, and detect malware. ML is used to detect fraudulent payments, protect the Cloud, and detect negotiated computers.

Many ML and AI systems have shown tremendous promise, but they have limitations. Attackers have started using ML as a threat. This is mainly done through data poisoning. The poisoning occurs if the attacker figures out how algorithms are set up, draws the training data, and introduces misleading data that builds a counter-narrative. This becomes a situation between legitimate data versus malicious data. This approach is used on a campaign of many accounts to mark malicious data as not spam, which can be misleading. The Cyxtera organization built an ML-based phishing generator that is trained on more than 100 million effective attacks. The system automatically generated scam and e-mails. The AI-based system bypassed the attacks by 15 percent with 0.3 percent accuracy.

AI Solutions for Federal Cybersecurity

Human beings have the tendency to experience and learn how to respond to situations. The same approach can be used to countermeasure security issues on computer systems. Collective knowledge and mastered trends can be used to respond to attacks with greater confidence, scale, and speed. An intelligent system such as ML and AI can be used to fight and beat security attacks.

New Trends With AI and Security

1. Evolution of AI bots for real-time adaptive security.
2. 2020 is predicted to have AI Bots protecting and attacking through AI bot intruders. This is going to be a challenging time for all organizations.
3. Every organization must implement AI solutions to mitigate the challenging time.

Cyber criminals will build systems that can learn and adapt to defense attacks.

- Worm: RPC vulnerability, disaster removal, and installed patches.
- Zombie: a malware strain that enslaves the IoT.

- Reaper and IoTroop: computer worms that are built to spread automatically.
- AI researchers warn that hundreds of Internet-connected robots are calling on governments to ban weaponized robots.
- Bots (computers that talk like humans such as Siri or Cortina, a computer program that completes automated tasks) are becoming one of the fastest growing trends with intelligent reasoning, messaging, and conversational interfaces. Intruders can bluff through these bots.

List of AI security capabilities:

- AI-bot capabilities
- ML
- Cyber-intelligence
- Behavioral analysis
- Ontology
- Understands entity state (posture)
- Orchestration and deception tactics
- Reactive AI-bots
- Reasoning AI-bots
- Chat with your bots software
- Creates talking knowledgebases for phone calls (Alexa).
- Enables increased accuracy

Data Protection

Useful data protection information is listed here:
https:// csoonline.com/

CSO Online

CSO provides state-of-the art information and best practices on business continuity, data protection, prevention of social engineering scams, malware, and breaches. CSO also provides tips and advice about security issues and leadership.

CHAPTER 4

Knowledgebase

Chapter Outline
- Define knowledgebase for the AI project
- Security knowledge development
- Objectives of the security Knowledgebase
- Identification of knowledge for security
- Knowledge acquisition for security
- Knowledge sharing

Key Learning Points
- Learn and understand knowledgebases
- Understand security knowledgebase development

Artificial Intelligence (AI) has intelligence that could be used repeatedly in applications with different needs. Corporate human resources have been tough for organizations (Albeado Inc. (Saratoga, C), 2019). Capturing and using the human intelligence required in organizations would be helpful. Captured knowledge and intelligence can be stored in the knowledgebase to build knowledge models, train the machines, and to use when necessary.

Capturing and using human intelligence requires an integrated information system. The idea is to develop an integrated system that provides the knowledge required by human experts. These integrated systems should be readily available and sharable. The integrated system should be used with strategic objectives in mind. This leads to the development of AI.

AI is used to solve important challenges based on the information stored in the knowledgebase. Human experts have cyclical demands in their subject matter expertise. Similar approaches are applied to management that are explored with use cases.

The knowledgebase stores data, techniques, and algorithms that will be used to drive the AI integrated system. The integrated system will be introduced gradually. The objective of the AI integrated system is to seek mitigation solutions for security in corporate settings. The objectives will consider using business rules that consist of "what if" questions. This uses strategic rules and logic to determine possible mitigation solutions using the stored data in the knowledgebase. The AI integrated system will impact knowledge objectives, identification of knowledge, knowledge acquisition, knowledge development, knowledge sharing, preservation of knowledge, fixing of knowledge, use of knowledge, evaluation of knowledge, and measurement of knowledge. The system will also impact the integration of AI case-based knowledge, representation of security cases, and the identification of similarities. AI connections are the building blocks of the knowledgebase. Bizstats.ai was built from scratch and turned into a full-blown AI integrated system using the knowledgebase.

Security Knowledge Development

The purpose of this section is to generate risk and security knowledge. This includes ideas, models, skills, processes, and methods that the system needs to train and learn. Machine learning (ML) can have various forms. Pattern-based learning is used in ML neural networks. This method gathers knowledge from a large amount of risk and security data, enabling the AI system to adapt when necessary.

Objectives of the Security Knowledgebase

Skills and knowledge must follow the appropriate corporate objectives in the Bizstats.ai security knowledgebase.

The objectives of security knowledgebase are as follows:

- To capture the threat and associated securities from the data, process, people, things (e.g., Internet of things), systems, and actions.
- To determine threat occurrence.

- To determine impact of threats.
- To determine a security threats priority.
- To allocate security owners.
- To determine security mitigation.
- To determine security action.
- To monitor security threat(s) continuously in real time and determine corrective action.
- To recommend security training and efficient security process(s).

Identification of Knowledge for Security

The corporate setting is used to model skills and knowledge to enable the AI to work well. This requires mapping the collected security knowledge. Every effort will be made to store the data in a form that enables the data to be retrieved correctly. This AI system allows access to collected data. Ultimately, the system should be able to build a corporate knowledgebase capable of being extended with new security data. The AI system has the ability to prevent any loss of information, retain, and update the security data. The system is automatically capable of building the knowledgebase and can search for additional information externally.

Knowledge Acquisition for Security

Security data will be collected using formal and informal channels. The data will be used internally and externally. The data collected will enable suitable competencies of the AI system. The data will ultimately come from experts and will be used with statistical, ML algorithms.

Knowledge Sharing

The purpose of security knowledge sharing is a critical part of the knowledge management cycle. It is important to realize that people, technology, and the corporate world are part of this phase. AI knowledge sharing solutions consist of machine intelligence that is capable of learning from other

AI systems using real-time API. Discovering trends in a specific area, such as security mitigation, can be effective. Another area where AI has been used efficiently is in the vehicle manufacturing industry. Humans do not need to go through the repetitive nature of using the data; the computer system does the job efficiently without overwhelming. Bizstats.ai has real-time API access to solve knowledge-sharing problems.

CHAPTER 5

AI Solutions for Security

- Discovery Phase
- Detect Phase
- Threat Score Phase
- Threat Response Phase
- Protect Phase
- Monitor Phase
- Conclusion
- Firms in AI Cybersecurity

Chapter Outline
- How to handle AI/ML models for security solutions

Key Learning Points
- Learn and understand how AI/ML applies to security areas
- Data preparation for
  o Input
  o Output
  o Training data
  o Validation data
- Evaluate different algorithms

Security AI Process

The artificial intelligence (AI) system being developed uses the following design approach:

- Discovery phase
- Detect phase

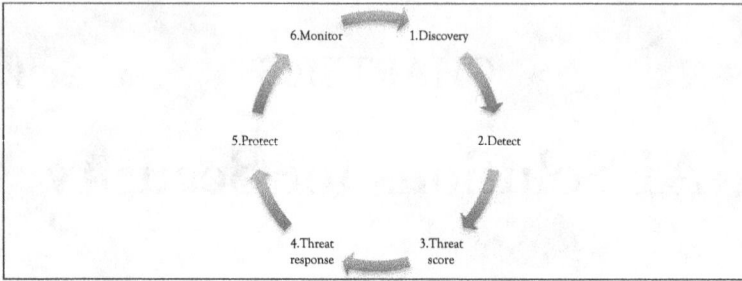

Figure 5.1 Security AI process

- Threat score phase
- Threat response phase
- Protect phase
- Monitor phase

See Figure 5.1. The necessary process is shown here.

Discover Phase

- Assets
  - o People
  - o Process
  - o Things and objects
  - o Technology
  - o Event
  - o Action
- Data
  - o Logs
  - o System and server
  - o Network activity
  - o Host
  - o Firewall
- Threats
  - o Entry point, end point, and edge
  - o Breaking to the system, host, and firewall
  - o Vulnerable assets
- Intrusion and violation
  - o Possible violation of assets

Detect Phase

- Signature-based detection (recognizing bad patterns such as malware).
- Anomaly-based detection [detecting deviations from a model of "good" traffic, which often relies on machine learning (ML)].

Threat Score

- Scoring the identified or detected threats.

Threat Response

- Identifying the best possible actions to be taken against the high-score threats.

Protect

- Take automatic actions or manual actions from the threat response phase.
- Example actions: block the IP, disable the user, or block all the access in the firewall.

Monitor

- Monitoring actions
- How often?
  - o Mostly real time
- Monitoring assets
  - o Monitoring people
  - o Monitoring processes
  - o Monitoring things and objects
  - o Monitoring technology
  - o Monitoring events
  - o Monitoring actions
  - o Monitoring data

  o Monitoring threats

  o Monitoring intrusions and violations

- Monitoring output
- Dashboard
- Score card
- Alerts (how critical the issue is)

This process helps companies address vulnerabilities and neutralize threats proactively instead of waiting for hackers to exploit high-security vulnerabilities.

The following sections will go through the AI process in detail.

Discover AI

Define Goal

- What assets pose serious threats?
- What assets are vulnerable?

Data Collection

Input:

- Table 5.1 illustrates sample assets in the organization.

Table 5.1 Assets in the organization

Device	IP Address	Type	Model
MacbookPro	192.168.2.100	Apple Mac	Apple MacBook Pro 2013
JohnDesktop	192.168.2.101	Computer	Windows XP
First Floor	192.168.2.102	Printer	HP Officejet 4650
Conference Room 1	192.168.2.103	Router	Netgear Nighthawk R7000

Table 5.2 Network traffic log

Event Time	Connection ID	Source IP/Port	Dest IP/Port	Data Transferred (bytes)	Bytes Uploaded (bytes)	Bytes Downloaded (bytes)	Flow Duration (sec)
Thu Sep 24 09:00	123123132	192.168.2.100: 4700	192.168.2.101: 80	23423423	2342234234	32423434	1029

- Table 5.2 illustrates network traffic connection logs, network metadata, and flow data (conversation between two hosts).
- Table 5.3 illustrates network metadata extracted features.

Table 5.3 Network metadata extracted features

Event Time	Connection ID	No. of Security Keywords	Min. Byte Value	Max. Byte Value	No. of Distinct Bytes	No. of Nonprint Chars	No. of Punctuation Chars
Thu Sep 24 09:00	123123132	3	4	9	100	3	5

- Network metadata additional extracted features:
  - These features can help the machine detect zero-day (before the actual attack happens) and web application attacks. See Table 5.4.

Table 5.4 Network metadata additional extracted features

Event Time	Connection ID	Contains Shell Code	Contains JavaScript Code	Contains SQL Command	Contains Command Injection
Thu Sep 24 09:00	123123132	Y	N	N	N

- Network metadata shellcode extracted features (advanced):
  - In hacking, a shellcode is a small piece of code used as the payload in the exploitation of a software vulnerability.
  - Extracted features are useful for detecting shellcode and malware. The shellcode is a bundle of codes or scripts that look like valid script. Shellcode typically starts as a command shell from which the attacker can control the compromised machine; however, any piece of code that performs a similar task can be called shellcode. See Table 5.5.

Table 5.5 Network metadata shellcode extracted features

Event Time	Connection ID	API Call Sequence
Thu Sep 24 09:00	123123132	1
Thu Sep 24 09:15	123123132	2

- Table 5.6 illustrates security events.

Table 5.6 Security events

Event Time	Event	Description	I/S	Source IP
Thu Sep 24 09:00	SV1	Local logon success	S	192.168.2.100
Thu Sep 24 09:15	SV2	Local logon fail	I	192.168.2.101
Thu Sep 24 09:15	SV3	Network traffic overload	I	192.168.2.101
Thu Sep 24 09:15	SV4	CPU usage overload	I	192.168.2.101
Thu Sep 24 09:15	SV5	Disk usage overload	I	192.168.2.101

- List of software with vulnerabilities:
  o Product, software, vendor, number of entries, software type, vulnerabilities, patches, compliance, and inventory.
- More features can be extracted using Natural Language Processing (NLP) techniques from structured and unstructured sources such as blog feeds, twitter feeds, and news feeds.

Output (label):
- Possibility of vulnerability
- Value: true or false

ML/AI use case:
This is a binary classification problem for list of all assets.

Design Algorithm

Binary classifiers can be used for this model.

Identify Features

From the above datasets, 11 of the most important and generic features are selected out of all features to train ML and AI models to recognize the vulnerable assets.

- Source IP
- Date
- Timestamp
- Time zone

- IP location
- Number of TCP/IP requests
- Number of requests with nonprintable characters
- Number of requests with punctuation characters
- Number of requests containing JavaScript
- Number of requests containing Structured Query Language (SQL) statement
- Number of requests containing command injection
- Number of API call sequences
- Number of failed security events
- Number of successful security events
- Number of vulnerable software installed
- Vulnerable (label and output)

Train the Model

Train the selected algorithms using the prepared dataset.

Tuning the hyperparameters to train the model.

Run the training multiple times with different combinations of the provided hyperparameters of batch size, epochs, optimizer, learn rate, momentum, and dropout rate to find the optimum combination of hyperparameters to determine the appropriate results.

- Batch size = [10, 20, 40, 60, 80, 100]
- epochs = [10, 50, 100]
- optimizer = ['SGD', 'RMSprop', 'Adagrad', 'Adadelta', 'Adam', 'Adamax', 'Nadam']
- learn rate = [0.001, 0.01, 0.1, 0.2, 0.3]
- momentum = [0.0, 0.2, 0.4, 0.6, 0.8, 0.9]
- dropout rate = [0.0, 0.1, 0.2, 0.3, 0.4, 0.5, 0.6, 0.7, 0.8, 0.9]

It is recommended to try out different combinations of hyperparameters using grid search.

Grid search = GridSearchCV(estimator=model, param_grid=param_grid, n_jobs=-1, scoring='accuracy')

Compare models with different hyperparameters and choose the best fit. Use the model to train further using the full dataset.

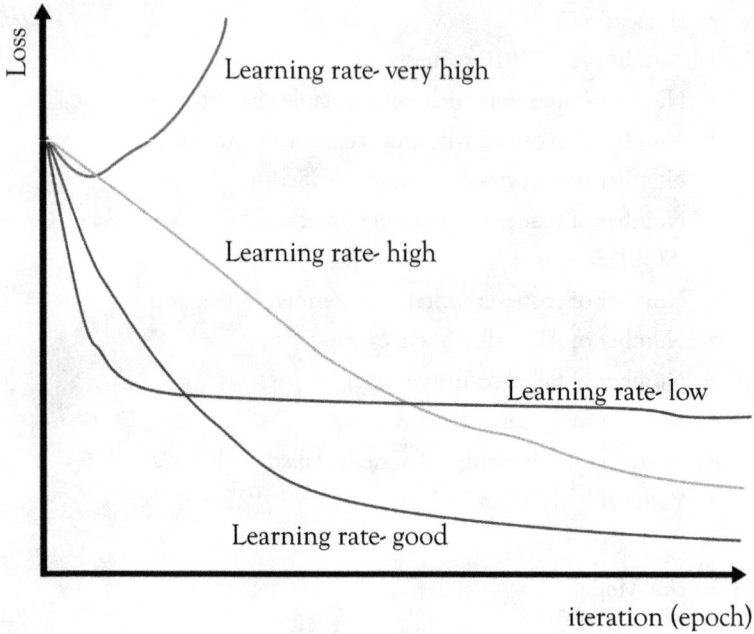

Figure 5.2 Loss versus epoch learning graph

Test the Model

Test the model using the test dataset for each selected algorithm with given methods:

- Specify the used loss function with respective algorithms
- Learning rate curve
- Learning curve

See Figure 5.2. Pick the model with the "Learning rate- Good," depicted in the graph.

Receiver Operating Characteristic Curve

Receiver operating characteristic curve is another common tool used with binary classifiers. See Figure 5.3. For this use case, let's choose the model with false positive rate of 0.99, since 90 percent accuracy is expected from Discover AI Model.

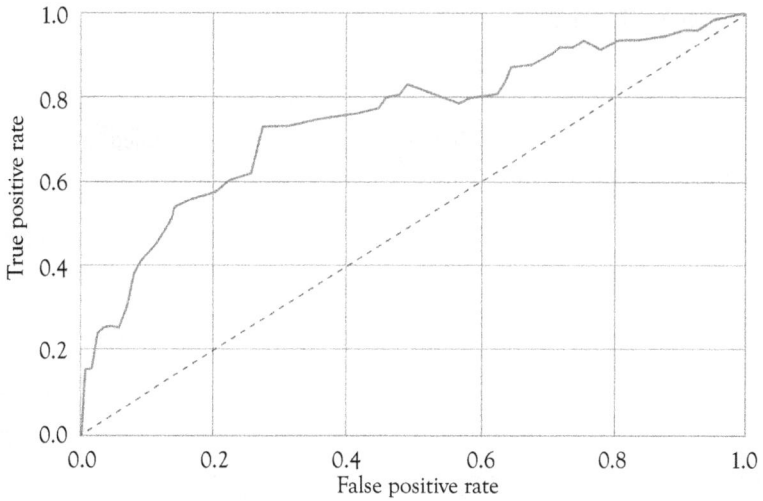

Figure 5.3 ROC curve

Evaluate the Model

Evaluate the model using accuracy and the mean square error (MSE) to determine the learning rate. The following scoring methods are used.

Scoring Methods

- Precision score
- Recall score
- F1 score
- Support score
- Accuracy score
- Area under the curve/receiver operating characteristic curve
- Learning rate (ranges from 0 to 1)

Confusion Matrix

- Analyze the inputs that are improperly classified using the confusion matrix.
- Note the accuracy versus epoch graph.
- Decide the final model with accuracy.

Repeat the steps from data collection, data preparation, feature extraction, training, testing, and evaluation of the model until the necessary accuracy of 85 and above is reached.

Table 5.7 shows the classification accuracy output obtained using several ML algorithms.

Table 5.7 Classification algorithm and accuracy

Naïve Bayer	81.5%
SVM	88.5%
J48	91%
Bayesian network	94%
Multinomial logistic regression	96.5%
FT (classifier for building "Functional Tree," classification trees that could have logistic regression functions at the inner nodes)	99.5%
SMO (implements John Platt's sequential minimal optimization algorithm for training a support vector classifier)	99.8%
Multilayer perceptron	100%

Model Conclusion

Based on the classification accuracy, multilayer perceptron is the best performing model for this binary classification problem.

Publish and Production of the Model

- Retrain the model until the desired output is reached.
  - o Repeat the steps from data collection, data preparation, feature extraction, training, testing, and evaluation, and then publish the model.
  - o Repeat the whole process for all the measures in this business process as explained in the evaluation steps.
- Here are the possible ways to produce the trained model:
  - o Host in Google Cloud, Microsoft Azure, or *Amazon Web Services* (AWS).
- How to deploy the trained model:
  - o https://Cloud.google.com/ml-engine/docs/tensorflow/deploying-models

- Regularly monitor and update the model.
- How to use the produced model for businesses:
  - o Integrate the trained model with the application so businesses can identify new securities or threats using the new dataset.

Conclusion

Type of resources needed for this project are as follows:

- Security threats analysis and subject matter expert
- Security threats mitigation strategists
- Data analysts
- Data architects
- Data scientists
- Data engineers

To simplify all the above steps, check out www.BizStats.AI
The automated steps are as follows:

- Provide input dataset
- Train multiple models
- Presented models with accuracy
- Pick and activate the model
- Use the model through a direct search.

Detect AI

Define Goal

Step 1: Detect the threats that have happened, are happening, or are going to happen
Step 2: Categorize the threat
- Categories
  - o User threat (phishing, ransomware)
  - o Application threat (cross-site scripting and SQL injection)

o Infrastructure threat (botnet, Trojan-DDoS)

o Operations risks

o Hardware risks

o Software risks

o Project risks

o Personnel risks

o Data risks

o Vendor risks

o Disaster and business continuity risks

o Compliance and security risks

Data Collection

Input the following (Table 5.8):

- Data from previous step.
- Vulnerable assets data from previous steps.
- Browser events (identification, date, user, PC, uniformed resource locator (URL), activity, and content).
- User security events [identification, date, user, PC, and activity (log on and logoff information)].
- Device events (identification, date, user, PC, file, tree, and activity).
- E-mail events (identification, date, user, PC, recipients, activity, size, attachments, and content).
- File events (identification, date, user, PC, filename, activity, to removable, from removable, and content).
- Decoy files (file name and PC).
- Employees list: (user first name and last name).
- Threat intelligence data (campaigns and attack patterns).
- File (dynamic link library and executable), static features [amount of byte randomness (entropy) in the text section, the number of sections, and the presence or absence of particular API calls].
- File dynamic features extracted by running it in the sandbox [central processing unit use (percentage), random access

memory use (count), swap memory use (count), received packets (count), received bytes (count), sent packets (count), sent bytes (count), and number of processes running (count)].

Table 5.8 Malwa attack data

Phishing URL	Targeted Brand	Time (UTC)
http://some...site.url/https.bb.de.jb/index1.html	Generic/Spear Phishing	17:43:24
http://some...site.url/https.bb.de.jb/index2.html	Generic/Spear Phishing	17:47:24
http://some...site.url/https.bb.de.jb	Generic/Spear Phishing	17:43:24

Output:
- Step 1
  - o Is it a threat or not?
  - o Values: yes or no
- Step 2
  - o What type of threat is this?
  - o Possible values: user threat, application threat, and infrastructure threat.
- ML and AI use case:
- Step 1
  - o It is a binary classification problem?
- Step 2
  - o This is a multiclass classification problem.

Design Algorithm

- Step 1
  - o Binary classifiers can be used for this model.
- Step 2
  - o Multiclass classifiers can be used for this model.

Identify Features

From the input datasets, the following features have been selected for this model:

Step 1: Detect the threat.

See Table 5.9.

Table 5.9 Detect the threat data sample

ID	Date	User	PC (mac address)	Event Type	Acti-vity	From	To	Size	Attach-ments	Con-tent	Threat
12w21	Thu Sep 24 09:00	john	sdf-dfdf-df-dfd-fd	E-mail	Sent	User	To, cc, bcc	10 MB	Yes	E-mail body	Y
w12d2	Thu Sep 24 09:00	smith	sdf-dfdf-df-dfd-fd	File	Down-load	Exter-nal device	Dest IP/ PC	100 MB	No	File con-tent	Y
wewd23	Thu Sep 24 09:00	chris	sdf-dfdf-df-dfd-fd	Browser	Http visit	URL	Dest IP/ PC	2 MB	No	Page con-tent	N
2dgfg34	Thu Sep 24 09:00	jen-nifer	sdf-dfdf-df-dfd-fd	User Secu-rity	Logon	-	Dest IP/ PC	-	No	-	N
32rffedc	Thu Sep 24 09:00	jack	sdf-dfdf-df-dfd-fd	Device	Con-nected	Exter-nal	Dest IP/ PC	10 GB	No	File tree	Y

Step 2: Categorize the threat. Only the threats are passed to this step.

See Table 5.10.

Table 5.10 Categorize the threat data sample

ID	Date	User	PC (mac address)	Event Type	Acti-vity	From	To	Size	Attach-ments	Content	Threat	Threat Category
12w21	Thu Sep 24 09:00	john	sdf-dfdf-df-dfd-fd	E-mail	Sent	User	To, cc, bcc	10 MB	Yes	E-mail body	Y	Insider threat
w12d2	Thu Sep 24 09:00	smith	sdf-dfdf-df-dfd-fd	Net-work	Files received	URL	Dest IP/ PC	100 MB	No	File content	Y	Application threat
32rffedc	Thu Sep 24 09:00	jack	sdf-dfdf-df-dfd-fd	Device	Con-nected	Exter-nal	Dest IP/ PC	10 GB	No	File tree	Y	User threat

Identify List of Algorithms

- Binary classification algorithms.
- Multiclass classification algorithms.
- Deep learning with unsupervised learning.
- Clustering
  - o Generally, this refers to the segregation of data into groups that have similar traits for the purpose of deciding a set of associated actions related to that grouping.

- o Clustering may be helpful in identifying security data from similar attack patterns by actors.
- Anomaly detection
  - o This is especially useful for identifying "unknown unknowns" such as zero-day threats.

Train the Model

Step 1: Detect the threat

This step is the same as the "Discover AI" step.

Step 2: Categorize the threat

Use the identified datasets to train the model.

- Split the dataset into three sets as illustrated below:
  - o Training dataset (60 percent)
  - o Test dataset (20 percent)
  - o Validation dataset (20 percent)
- Tune the hyperparameters to train the model as done to Discover AI models.
- Train the model for multiple iterations with 100 epochs per iteration.
- Train the model for various combinations of features to find the best model.

Tune the Model

Tune the hyperparameters to train the model.

Run the training multiple times with different combinations of the hyperparameters of selected algorithms. This typically includes batch size, epochs, optimizer, learn rate, momentum, and dropout rate to find the optimum combination of hyperparameters to determine the appropriate results.

Compare models with different hyperparameters and choose the best fit. Then, use the model to train using the full dataset.

Test the Model

Step 1 is the same as the "Discover AI" step.

Step 2 is the same as the "Discover AI" step, except it uses a multiclass classification.

Evaluate the Model

Step 1 is the same as the "Discover AI" step.
Step 2: Categorize the threat

Evaluate the model using accuracy, MSE, and determine the learning rate.

Use Confusion Matrix

Confusion matrix measures the performance of the classification algorithms. See Figure 5.4.

Confusion matrix graph for multiclass classification:

- X: Predicted value [security categories], 5 (1 to 5).
- Y: Targeted value [target categories], 5 (1 to 5).

Use encoded values instead of actual security categories.

Precision–Recall Curves

Precision–recall curves measure the success of the classification model.
See Figure 5.5.

	Catagory A	Catagory B	Catagory C	Catagory D	Catagory E	
Catagory A	70	5	7	9	9	100
Catagory B	2	77	6	8	7	
Catagory C	4	4	80	5	7	50
Catagory D	7	3	2	79	9	
Catagory E	2	5	3	18	72	0

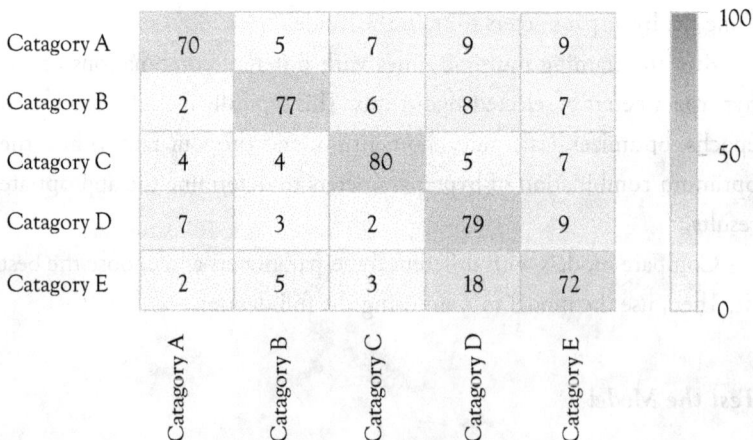

Figure 5.4 Confusion matrix predicted versus targeted

Precision and recall Vs K (expanded user-item matrix)

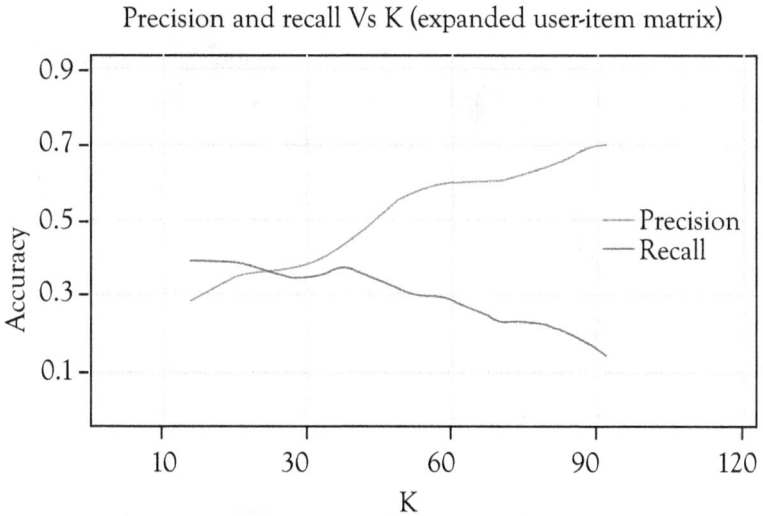

Figure 5.5 Precision and recall versus K

Check mistakes of the classification model on each label and analyze to fine-tune (see Figure 5.6).

Decide the final model with accuracy

- If the classification prediction is wrong, you can improve the accuracy by using more training data. Therefore, collect more data then retrain the classification and reevaluate the model for the improvement on the accuracy.

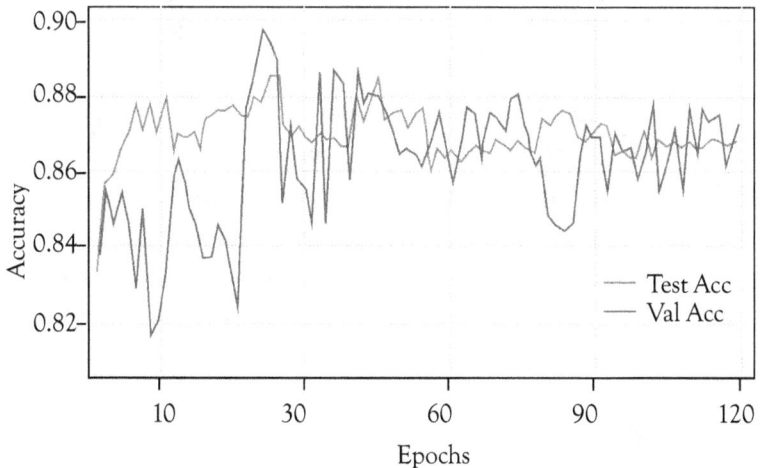

Figure 5.6 Accuracy versus epoch graph

- If the case is "classification prediction is wrong because of wrong training data," use urAI-text annotation tool (https://bizstats.ai/product/urAI.html) to correct the input training data, then retrain the classification and reevaluate the model for the improvement on the accuracy.
  - o Another method of evaluating the model accuracy is to use ensemble learning methods.

The ensemble learning methods are as follows:
  - o Sequential ensemble methods.
  - o Parallel ensemble methods.
  - o Combination of both.
  - o Weighted majority rule ensemble classifier.

Based on our experiments, the finalized ensemble classifier method is "weighted majority rule ensemble classifier." This provides better accuracy than any other ensemble methods.

Weighted Majority Rule Ensemble Classifier

Three different classification models can be used to classify the samples: logistic regression, a naive Bayes classifier with a Gaussian kernel, and a random forest classifier all combined into an ensemble method.

- Cross-validation (five-fold cross-validation) results provide the following:
  - o Accuracy: 0.90 (±0.05) [logistic regression].
  - o Accuracy: 0.92 (±0.05) [random forest].
  - o Accuracy: 0.91 (±0.04) [naïve Bayes].

The cross-validation results show that the performance of the three models is almost equal.

A simple ensemble classifier class can be implemented to combine the three different classifiers. A predict method simply takes the majority rule of the predictions by the classifiers. Here are some examples:

- Classifier 1 to class 1.
- Classifier 2 to class 1.
- Classifier 3 to class 2.

Table 5.11 Weighted average calculation

Classifier Name	Class 1	Class 2	Class 3
Classifier 1	W1 * 0.2	W1 * 0.5	W1 * 0.3
Classifier 2	W1 * 0.6	W1 * 0.3	W1 * 0.1
Classifier 3	W1 * 0.3	W1 * 0.4	W1 * 0.3
Weighted average	0.37	0.4	0.3

Now, classify the sample as "class 1."

Furthermore, adding a weights parameter assigns a specific weight to each classifier. To work with the weights, collect the predicted class probabilities for each classifier, multiply it by the classifier weight, and take the average based on these weighted average probabilities. Next, one must assign the class label.

To illustrate this with a simple example, let us assume to have three classifiers and three-class classification problems to assign equal weights to all classifiers (the default): w1 = 1, w2 = 1, w3 = 1.

The weighted average probabilities for a sample would be calculated as follows (see Table 5.11).

The class 2 has the highest weighted average probability; thus, the sample is classified as class 2.

- Accuracy: 0.90 (±0.05) [logistic regression].
- Accuracy: 0.92 (±0.05) [random forest].
- Accuracy: 0.91 (±0.04) [naive Bayes].
- Accuracy: 0.95 (±0.03) [ensemble].

The ensemble classifier class is used to apply to majority voting using the class labels if no weights are provided and the predicted probability values show otherwise (see Table 5.12).

Table 5.12 Prediction based on majority class label

Classifier Name	Class 1	Class 2
Classifier 1	1	0
Classifier 1	0	1
Classifier 1	0	1
Prediction	-	1

Table 5.13 Weighted average with prediction

Classifier	Class 1	Class 2
Classifier 1	0.99	0.01
Classifier 2	0.49	0.51
Classifier 3	0.49	0.51
Weighted average	0.66	0.18
Prediction	1	-

Prediction based on predicted probabilities:

This is for equal weights: weights = [1, 1, 1]. See Table 5.13.

The results are different depending on whether a majority vote based on the class labels or the average of the predicted probabilities is applied. In general, it makes more sense to use the predicted probabilities (scenario 2). Here, "very confident" classifier 1 overrules the very unconfident classifiers 2 and 3.

A naive brute-force approach should be used to find the optimal weights for each classifier to increase the prediction accuracy.

The results look nice when applying the ensemble classifier (see Table 5.14). One must keep in mind that this is just a toy example. The majority rule voting approach might not always work so well in practice, especially if the ensemble consists of more "weak" than "strong" classification models. This uses a cross-validation approach to overcome the overfitting challenge, please always keep a spare validation dataset to evaluate the results.

Model Conclusion

Step 1 is the same as the "Discover AI" step.
Step 2: Categorize the threat.

Table 5.14 Example of compare table

Iteration	W1	W2	W3	Mean	Standard Deviation
2	1	2	2	0.953333	0.033993
17	3	1	2	0.953333	0.033993
20	3	2	2	0.946667	0.045216

Based on our experiment, the "weighted majority rule ensemble classifier" performs better than other algorithms for the "Detect AI: Categorize the threat model."

Publishing and Production of Models

Step 1 is the same as the "Discover AI" step.
Step 2 is the same as the "Discover AI" step.

Conclusion

Step 1 is the same as the "Discover AI" step.
Step 2 is the same as the "Discover AI" step.

Threat Score AI

Define Goal

Score the identified threats for prioritization of issues for further investigation.

Data Collection

Input:

- Identified threats from step "Detect AI."
- List of historical threats and their impact.
- External security events data.
- Blogs, articles, and news to understand the threat and its impact.

Output:

- Threat score (1–10).
- Continuous output variable.

ML and AI use case:
  This is a regression problem.

Table 5.15 Threat score data sample

Event ID	Threat Type	Threat Impact (in dollars)	Likelihood of Exploi-tation (%)	Number of Social Media Shares	Level of Inter-connected-ness With Other Assets (%)	Does it Impact Critical Business Operation?	Size of User Base	Threat Score
wewd23	Hacking	5M	20	3k	20	Y	500	5
12w21	Data theft	24M	10	10k	15	Y	5M	8
w12d2	Cross-site scripting	2M	50	4k	25	N	100	3

Design Algorithm

Regression algorithms can be used for this model.

Identify Features

See Table 5.15.

Train the Model

Using Deep Neural Network Architecture

The deep neural network can be trained to predict the threat score (see Figure 5.7).

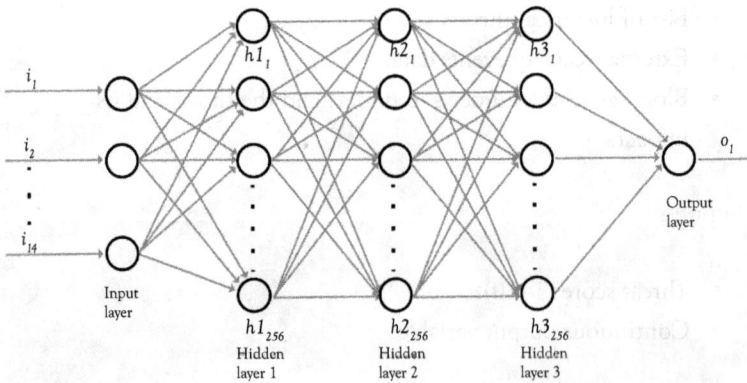

Figure 5.7 Fully connected neural network layer for deep neural networks

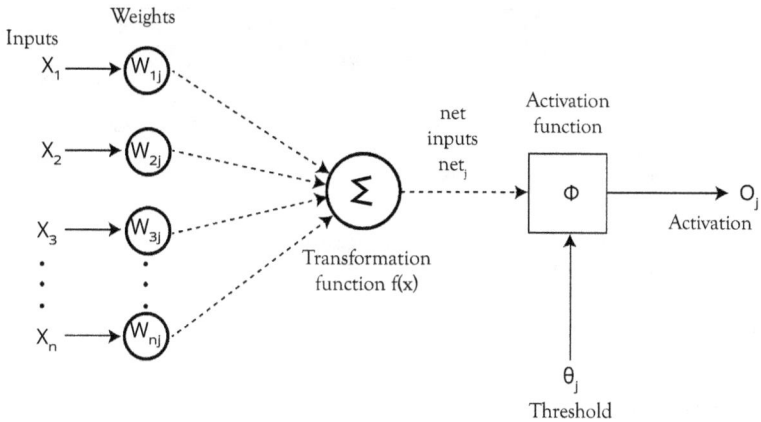

Figure 5.8 Activation function of neural network

Fully connected neural network layers consist of a list of inputs into a list of outputs. Three basic types of layers exist: input layers, output layers, and hidden layers. The functionality-based layers are convolution layers, maximum and average pooling layers, dropout layer, nonlinearity layer, loss function layers, and much more (see Figure 5.8).

This deep neural network consists of

- One input layer with 14 nodes.
- Three hidden layers with 256 nodes each with a ReLU activation function and a normal initializer, such as the kernel initializer.
- Mean absolute error as a loss function.
- Output layer with only one node.
- Use "linear" as the activation function for the output layer.

See Table 5.16.

Table 5.16 Deep neural network layers

Layer (type)	Output Shape	Param #
Input layer (Dense)	(none, 128)	19,200
Hidden layer 1 (Dense)	(none, 256)	33,024
Hidden layer 1 (Dense)	(none, 256)	65,792
Hidden layer 1 (Dense)	(none, 256)	65,792
Output layer (Dense)	(none, 1)	257
Total params: 184,065; trainable params: 184,065; non-trainable params: 0.		

```
[out]:
Train on 1168 samples, validate on 292 samples
Epoch 1/500
1168/1168 [==========================] - 0s 266us/step -loss:
19251.8903 - mean_absolute_error: 19251.8903 - val_loss: 23041.8968
- val_mean_absolute_error: 23041.8968
Epoch 0001: val_loss did not improve from 21730.9355
Epoch 2/500
1168/1168 [==========================] - 0s 268us/step -loss:
19251.8903 - mean_absolute_error: 18300.8433 - val_loss: 22324.8762
- val_mean_absolute_error: 21231.8968
Epoch 0002: val_loss did not improve from 21730.9355

.
.
.

Epoch 0500: val_loss did not improve from 18520.2376
```

Figure 5.9 Training log output

The validation loss of the best model is 18520.23 (see Figure 5.9).

Using Other Algorithms

Use the identified datasets to train the model.

Fit a model using linear regression first and then determine whether the linear model provides an adequate fit by *checking the residual plots.* If a good fit cannot be obtained using linear regression, try a nonlinear model because it can fit a wider variety of curves. It is recommended to use ordinary least squares (OLS) first because OLS is easier to perform and interpret.

Use Akaike's information criterion (AIC), Bayesian information criterion (BIC) (see Figure 5.10), or Mallows' CP to decide how many factors should be used. These methods are better than comparing with R2.

Use multiple regression. If the sample size is large enough, you may use autoselect option such as forward backward or best. This option will select independent factors using sampling techniques.

Test the Model

Test the model using the test dataset and expert knowledge.

Analyzing different metrics like statistical significance of parameters, R-square, adjusted r-square, and AIC, model is considered to be more

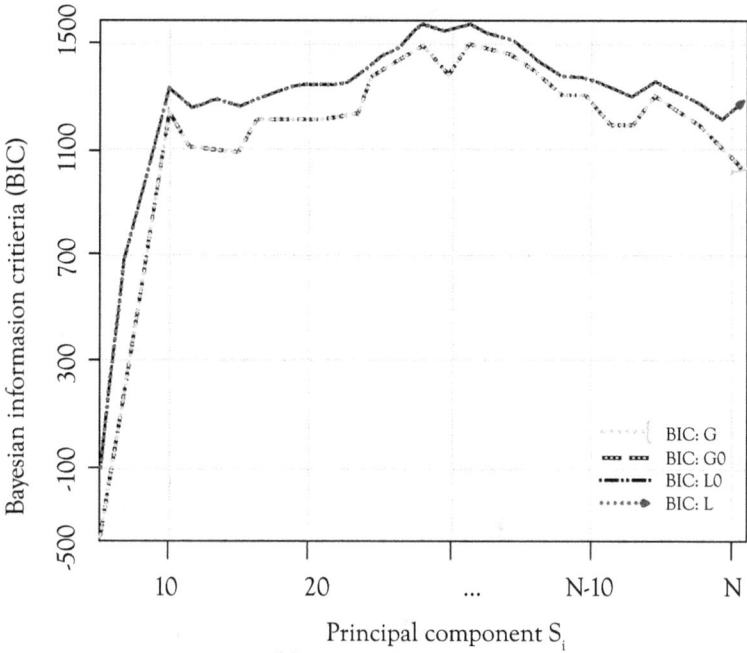

Figure 5.10 Principal components versus Bayesian information criterion

likely to be the true model (BIC) and error term. Another one is the *Mallow's Cp* criterion. This checks for possible bias in your model by comparing the model with all possible submodels (or a careful selection of them). See Figure 5.11.

The model is more accurate for the left graph.

You should not choose automatic model selection methods if your dataset has multiple confounding variables because you do not want to put these in a model at the same time. Regression regularization methods

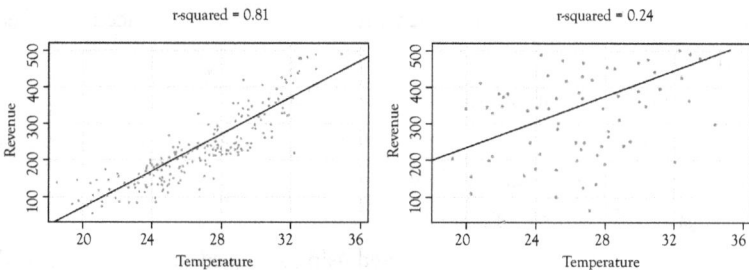

Figure 5.11 R-squared comparison graph

Good vs bad ML cross validation

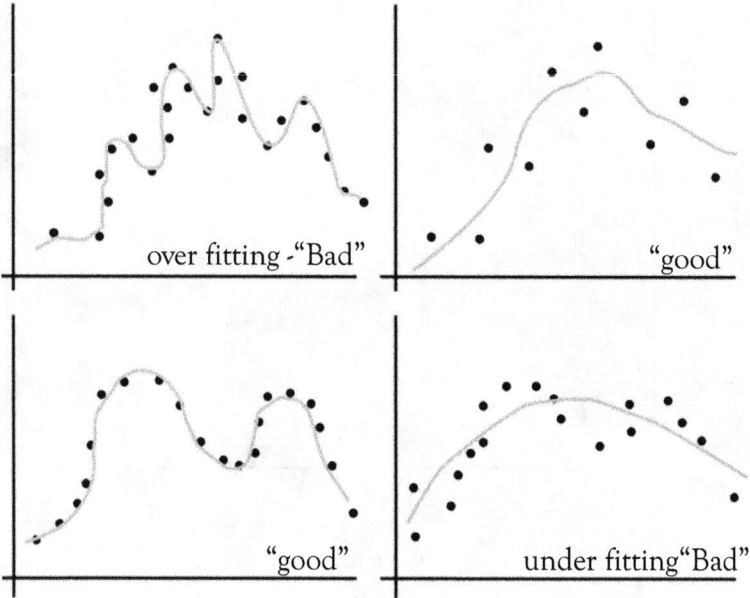

Figure 5.12 Cross-validation comparison

work well in case of high dimensionality and multicollinearity among the variables in the dataset.

Evaluate the Model

Evaluate the model using accuracy and MSE to determine the learning rate. Cross-validation is the best way to evaluate models used for prediction. Cross-validation divides your dataset into two groups (train and validate). A simple mean squared difference between the observed and predicted values gives you a measure for the prediction accuracy. See Figure 5.12.

Predicting threat score model using linear model:

See Figure 5.13 for the predicted versus the actual and root mean square error (RMSE) score below.

Test RMSE score: 5.125877.

The threat score model is predicted using a bagged model. The bagged model is fitted using the randomForest algorithm. Bagging is a special

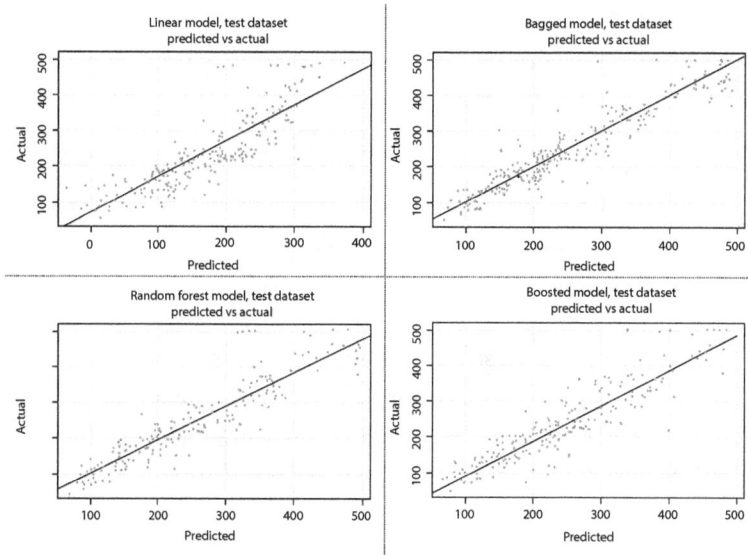

Figure 5.13 Evaluate ensemble model predicted versus actual

case of a random forest where mtry (number of variables randomly sampled as candidates at each split) is equal to p, the number of predictors. Try using 13 predictors. Test RMSE score: 3.843966.

The model provides two interesting results. First, the predicted versus the actual plot no longer has a small number of predicted values. Second, our test error has dropped dramatically. Also note that the "mean of squared residuals," which is output by randomForest, is the out of bag estimate of the error. For regression, the suggestion is to use mtry equal to $p/3 = 4$ predictors. Test RMSE score: 3.701805.

Here note the three RMSEs: the training RMSE (which is optimistic), the out-of-bag (OOB) RMSE (which is a reasonable estimate of the test error), and the test RMSE. Also note that the variables' importance was calculated. See Table 5.17.

Table 5.17 Data versus error comparison

No	Data	Error
1	Training Data	1.558111
2	OOB	3.576229
3	Test	3.701805

Table 5.18 Test error score of each model

	Model	Test Error
1	Single Tree	5.45808
2	Linear Model	5.12587
3	Bagging	3.84396
4	Random Forest	3.70180
5	Boosting	3.43382

Lastly, try using a boosted model. This model produces a nice variable importance plot and plots the marginal effects of the predictors. Based on this analysis, decide which variables most influence the threat score. See Table 5.18.

Model Conclusion

Ensemble boosting model performed better than other algorithms for predicting threat score models.

Publishing and Production of Model

This is the same as the "Discover AI" step.

Conclusion

The same ML and AI model can be used for scoring the skills mentioned below.

Skills AI scoring models:

1. Respectfulness score (helping others retain their autonomy)
2. Courteousness score
3. Friendliness score
4. Kindness score
5. Honesty score
6. Trustworthy score
7. Loyalty score
8. Ethical score

The skills scoring models can be used with customers, customer support executives, project resources, vendors, suppliers, buyers, and much more.

Threat Response AI

Define Goal

Predict what response needs to be taken to fix the threat.

Data Collection

Input:

- Identify threats using the score from Discover AI, Detect AI, and Threat Score AI.
- Other inputs from Discover AI, Detect AI, and Threat Score AI.
  - o Categories of threat
    - Human threats: Malicious human activity can be a major threat to your computer. For example, a discontented employee may try to tamper with or destroy data on an employer's computer. A hacker is someone who tries to access your computer illegally via the Internet.
    - Processes
    - Things and objects
    - Technologies
    - Events
    - Actions
- List of historical threat responses and their impact.

Output:

- Predict what action needs to be taken toward the present threat.
- Values
  - o Block
    - Determine whether there is a need to respond to the source of the event (e.g., blocking the source).

o Deceive
  • Determine whether there is a need to respond in a manner that causes further action and events (e.g., modifying the response to the source so that it can learn more about the threats behavior).
o Apply fix
  • Determine whether there is a need to fix the issues of the event (e.g., applying patch for the operating system).
o No action
  • Determine whether there is a need to consider action at all (e.g., determine if the event is relevant to the environment or if it should remain unknown that the source has been detected).

ML and AI Use case:

This is a multiclass classification problem

Design Algorithm

This is the same as the "Detect AI: Categorize the threat" step.

Identify Features

This is the same as the "Detect AI: Categorize the threat" step.

Train the Model

This is the same as the "Detect AI: Categorize the threat" step.

Test the Model

This is the same as the "Detect AI: Categorize the threat" step.

Evaluate the Model

This is the same as the "Detect AI: Categorize the threat" step.

Model Conclusion

This is the same as the "Detect AI: Categorize the threat" step.

Publish/Production of Model

This is the same as the "Detect AI: Categorize the threat" step.

Conclusion

This is the same as the "Detect AI: Categorize the threat" step.

Protect AI

Define Goals

- Stop anomalous activity in real time: at the point of access.
- Take action automatically or notify users based on the threat response and AI output.

Data Collection

Input:
- Output of step "Threat Response AI."
- List of historical protected and unprotected logs.
- Knowledge about previous protection steps.
- Protection rules.

Output:
- Action report.
- Automated steps needed to protect.
- If it is manual, provide the instruction steps needed to protect.
- Suggested action.
- Block the asset (e.g., remove the vulnerable desktop from network using mac address).
- Block the user (e.g., disable the user from logging into the network using username or other identification).

Design Algorithm

The following algorithms can be used for this model:

- Decision tree
- Reinforcement learning

Identify Features

Prepare data from the available input dataset and from the "Threat Response AI" step.

Train the Model

This is the same as the "Detect AI: Categorize the threat" step.

Test the Model

This is the same as the "Detect AI: Categorize the threat" step.

Evaluate the Model

This is the same as the "Detect AI: Categorize the threat" step.

Model Conclusion

This is the same as the "Detect AI: Categorize the threat" step.

Publish/Production of Model

This is the same as the "Detect AI: Categorize the threat" step.

Conclusion

This is the same as the "Detect AI: Categorize the threat" step.

Monitor AI

Define Goals

- Security monitoring:
  - o Constantly monitors the security level of your assets, users, and external IPS to identify your greatest threats. Reviews historical alerts using probabilistic models to identify assets and uncovers deeper links between alerts and existing rules-based systems.
- Network threat detection technology:
  - o Understands traffic patterns on the network and monitors traffic in and between trusted networks, as well as Internet traffic.
- Recover:
  - o Continuously monitors and learns from the data it collects from various data. Recovery can provide a user-role assignment recommendation based on the least privileged model.
- Detect
  - o Continuously monitors the near real-time event stream and detects anomalous behavior and potential threats with a threat detection engine. This engine uses big data analytics and real-time ML algorithms to automatically identify the risks from massive amounts of access event data and access entitlements data. Risky events are annotated with security scores as well as the security distribution and alerts are created.

Monitor in Discover Phase

This is done using dashboards and scorecards.

Monitor in Detect Phase

This is done using dashboards and scorecards.

Monitor in Threat Scoring Phase

This is done using dashboards and scorecards.

Monitor in Threat Response Phase

This is done using dashboards and scorecards.

Monitor in Protect Phase

This is done using dashboards and scorecards.

Firms in AI Cybersecurity

The development of AI techniques has seen AI appear in a lot of different IT products, including the field of cybersecurity. Here are some key innovators in cybersecurity that are using AI to give their products an edge (Cooper 2019).

1. Darktrace
2. Cynet
3. FireEye
4. Check Point
5. Symantec
6. Sophos
7. Fortinet
8. Cylance
9. Vectra

AI is becoming popular throughout the world and is being included in many software applications, especially in cybersecurity products.

The following organizations are spearheading the initiatives with AI cybersecurity applications:

Darktrace: When initially installed, Darktrace creates a baseline as a protection point. From the baseline, any unusual occurrence on the network is treated as a threat. The detection of an anomaly triggers an automated response, which also relies on AI technology.

Cynet: This application is installed on the network to provide accessible threat protection to organizations that do not have specialist cybersecurity personnel.

FireEye: This company produces cybersecurity tools that use AI to monitor networks and spot anomalies. FireEye manages detection response and incident response.

Check Point: Check Point is invested in the development of three AI-driven platforms that contribute to many key offerings in business. These offerings are Campaign Hunting, Huntress, and Context-Aware Detection.

Symantec: This is a targeted attack analytics tool. The innovative deployment of AI by the company makes it a good blend of capital-increasing security and savings-defending stability.

Sophos: The two main AI-based Sophos products are Intercept X for endpoint protection and the XG Firewall to protect networks. Intercept X uses AI to avoid the need for a threat database distributed from a central location. It uses a deep learning neural network developed by Invincea.

Fortinet: One of Fortinet's products is FortiGate, a hardware firewall. This application is a workflow that includes endpoint protection, access protection, application monitoring (such as e-mail and web security), and advanced threat protection.

Cylance: All of Cylance's products integrate AI technology. Its main packages are:

- Cylance Protect: an endpoint security system.
- Cylance Optics: a corporate version of Cylance Protect. Threat detection is applied to all devices on the system and stored centrally.
- Cylance Threat Zero: Consultants propose a blend of products and can also customize protection software.
- Cylance Smart Antivirus: This is an AI-based AV system suitable for home users and small businesses.

Vectra: This is a threat detection system that deploys AI methodologies to establish a baseline of activity throughout an enterprise and

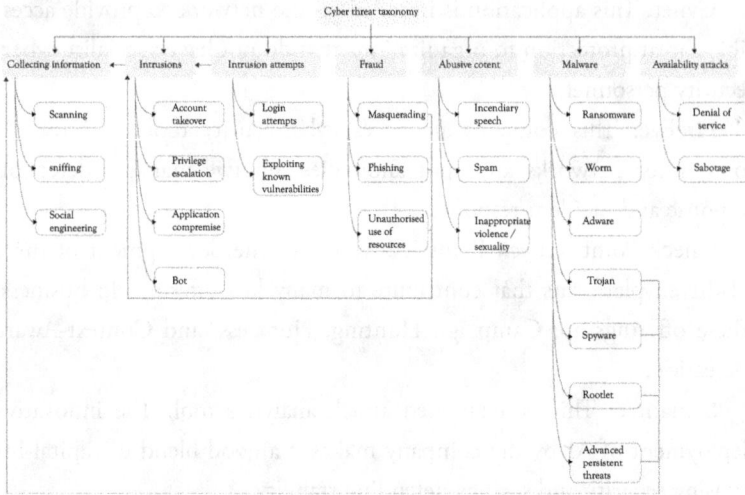

Figure 5.14 Cyber threat taxonomy

identify anomalies. See Figure 5.14 to view possible cyberattacks that are known currently.

See Figure 5.15.

| Behavior based |
| Reverse engineering and binary analysis for malicious behaviors. Requires no previous knowledge of malware. Effective at detecting files attacks |

| Threat intelligence |
| Matchmaking or extrapolating observations based on known threat data. Requires that threat intel be available. |

| Containerzaion |
| Available for small number of applications, mainly browsers, does not detect threats outside of the sandbox. |

| Next gen antivirus |
| Machine learning based. On-disk static file analysis. Requires frequent updates to ML model. Limited against fileless attacks. |

| Antivirus |
| Signature based. On-disk static file analysis. Required frequent update. Detects only known threats. |

Figure 5.15 Cybersecurity types that are known

Asset Discovery

Asset discovery will find and provide you visibility into the assets in your AWS, Azure, and on-premises environments. You will be able to discover all the IP-enabled devices on your network, determining what software and services are installed on them, how they are configured, and whether there are any vulnerabilities or active threats being executed against them.

What instances are running in my Cloud environments?

What devices are on my physical and virtual networks?

What vulnerabilities exist on the assets in my Cloud and network?

What are my users doing?

Are there known attackers trying to interact with my Cloud and network assets?

Are there active threats on my Cloud and network assets?

Intrusion Detection

Intrusion detection detects any intrusion threats as they emerge in your critical Cloud and on-premises infrastructure.

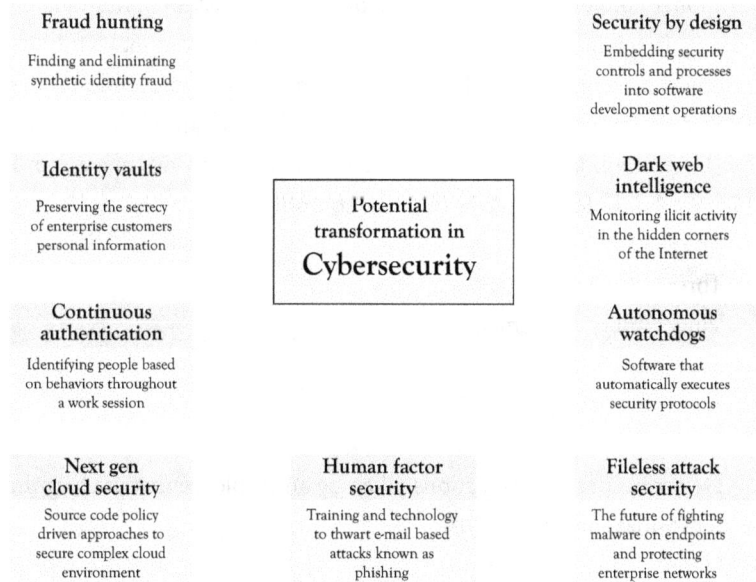

Fraud hunting

Finding and eliminating synthetic identity fraud

Security by design

Embedding security controls and processes into software development operations

Identity vaults

Preserving the secrecy of enterprise customers personal information

Potential transformation in Cybersecurity

Dark web intelligence

Monitoring ilicit activity in the hidden corners of the Internet

Continuous authentication

Identifying people based on behaviors throughout a work session

Autonomous watchdogs

Software that automatically executes security protocols

Next gen cloud security

Source code policy driven approaches to secure complex cloud environment

Human factor security

Training and technology to thwart e-mail based attacks known as phishing

Fileless attack security

The future of fighting malware on endpoints and protecting enterprise networks

Figure 5.16 Potential transformation in cybersecurity that are applying AI use cases

Security domain				Viruses Worms Spam
Network components Web applications End point computer Messaging Internet service provider	Data leakage Denial of service Information loss Personality theft Loss of confidentiality	Executable Text file E-mail IP-packet XML file	End point antivirus Network antivirus Signature based filter Anti spam system	D.O.S attacks Buffer overflow SQL injection Misues System intrusion
Threat domain	**Damage type**	**Raw data type**	**Proactive security**	**Threat type**

Computer security
using
machine learning

Analysis type	Learning algorithm	Feature selection	Extracted features
Static Dynamic Sequence	Supervised Unsupervised Semi-supervised	Gain ratio Fisher score Document frequency Hierarchical feature Document frequency	Function based Sting signature Network trafic Time series n-grams OpCode n-grams XML features Packet header

Machine learning domain

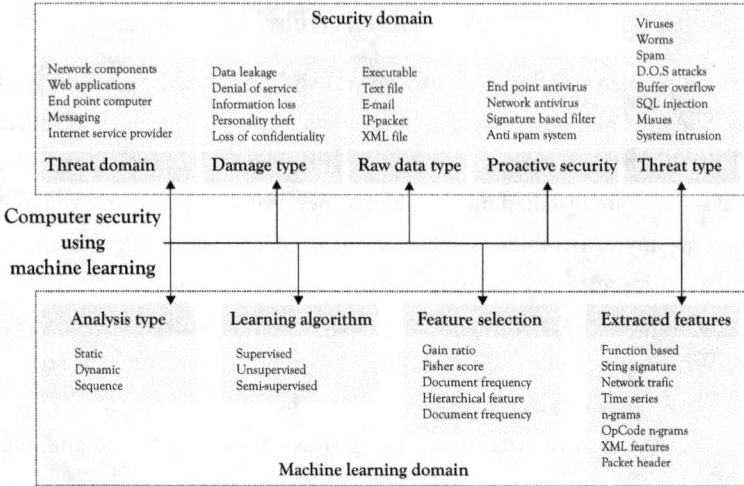

Figure 5.17 Computer security using ML that explains how security domains maps to ML domains

Endpoint Detection and Response

Corporate endpoints represent one of the top areas of security for organizations. As malicious actors increasingly design their attacks to evade traditional endpoint prevention and protection tools, organizations are looking to endpoint detection and response for additional visibility, including evidence of attacks that might not trigger prevention rules. While many security teams recognize the need for advanced threat detection for endpoints, most do not have the resources to manage a standalone endpoint detection and response solution.

Threat Detection

Threat Intelligence

Vulnerability Assessment

See Figure 5.16.

See Figure 5.17.

Goal:

Detect insider threats: actions taken by an employee that are harmful to an organization:

Unsanctioned data transfer.

Sabotage of resources.

Misuse of network that disrupts the organization.

Input:

File event: event identification, file name, file type, action (copied), and size.

E-mail: event identification, date, user, recipients, activity (send), size, attachments, and content.

Http event: event identification, date, user, and URL.

CHAPTER 6

Industry Domain

Purpose

- This chapter looks at different industry domains
- How industries are impacted by security
- How security can be applied to industry domains

Chapter Outline

- Insurance security management
- Disaster security management
- Credit and financial industry
- Auto industry
- Health security management
- Government privacy security

Key Learning Points

- Learn and understand how industry domains have security-related threats, learn how to apply AI, and understand where AI is heading.

Insurance Security Management

Impacts that benefit customers are heavily considered in the insurance security management assessment and the quantification of probability and financial security (Faiier et al. 2019). The customer financial settlement must weigh in. This discussion covers insurance guaranteeing in the insurance industry. Insurance organization security will require security management to understand the business risks that are identified, analyzed, engineered, reduced, eliminated, or transferred. Insurance is often the final transfer of risk. Some risks require insurance solutions such as large liability limits for some targeted products. An example could be automobile exposures and varied products.

Obtaining insurance for some assets will help reduce risk for both insurance organizations and policyholders' benefits. Insurance companies play a role in identifying activities related to the customer assets in question. This can result in a claim filed by the customer that may result in paid claims and other losses. Insurance may not pay for the complete customer loss.

Disaster Security Management

Disasters are difficult and can hurt different people. Disaster hurts the vulnerable and the poor, who have little or no defenses (Bronfman, Cisternas, Repetto, and Castañeda 2019). Storm-related vulnerabilities cause fatality in lower-income countries. Some statistical numbers show that in over 30 years, approximately 2.5 million people have died due to natural disasters. These are sad statistics that do not need to be repeated.

Almost 75 percent of disasters are created by weather events and climate threats (Shaw 2011). Disasters create poverty. On another note, the rapid growth of population is leading to an increase in disaster risks. This trend is caused by city's lack of investment in resilient infrastructure. Mainstream security management will reverse the trend of rising disaster impact. Additionally, people's livelihood and well-being will improve by planning and building stronger infrastructure. This will potentially cut global losses.

Countries need to be proactive to save lives and assets. Unfortunately, some developing countries lack the tools, expertise, and instruments to make adequate investment decisions.

Credit and Financial Management

Credit security management has been studied for decades and shows a significant performance effect on commercial banks (Feldman 2019).

A study focused on nonperforming loans and total assets showed a significant relationship between bank performance and credit security management.

Further study outcome showed the return on equity and return on assets were used as performance indicators, and nonperforming loans and credit adequate ration were also used. The result showed that credit security management has a significant impact on commercial banking.

Auto Industry

Security analysis in the automobile industry has shown that security threats can be associated with specific circumstances (Kunkle 2019). Security in the auto industry must be identified and mitigated. The opposite may lead to production loss as well as safety measures. India has studied auto industry risks in-depth. Tools such as Bayesian Networks for assessment are used.

Different car industries have effective sales, while other manufacturers are not as successful. The Indian government proactively began researching the risks associated with the auto industry. The findings from the research showed that 7.1 percent of India's Gross Domestic Product and approximately 29,000,000 Indian citizens are employed. Subsequent analysis indicated that India rose to fourth largest manufacturer and seventh largest manufacturer of commercial vehicles in the world. The assessment indicated that there is a rise in risk, and this requires taking higher security measures.

Three risks emerged from the auto industry. Currently, the auto industry has electronic and self-driving cars. This comes with some risks, and may lead to loss of production targets and vehicle recalls if not evaluated. Here are the security issues that can hurt the industry: customer's constant demanding (aggressive demand of different cars), economic risks (the cost of making cars is higher than the profit of selling them), and security of disruption (the competition is no longer easy for the industry).

The above risks are problems that the industry needs to evaluate and control. Security management can be improved by applying safety measures, manufacture product quality, obsolete product, and security measures. It is important to take precaution instead of waiting for risks to occur.

Health Security Management

Health security management is concerned with patient health care risks (Boland and O'Riordan 2019; Blass 2019). The risks extend to the staff and the entire health organization. The organization is better if the specific staff is trained in handling likely risks that may occur in the organization environment. Trained staff will be able to identify risks, develop security strategies, implement planned strategies, and subsequently monitor likely risks and security issues.

Trained staff will handle varied issues, including working proactively and reactively to prevent an incident or to minimize damages. The trained staff will typically work in the following areas: clinical research, emergency preparedness, psychological and human health care, event and incident management, financing, insurance, and management.

Health security management is concerned with patient health care risks. The staff will work to reduce risks that consist of patients, staff members, and visitors. This requires a continuous security assessment to decrease risks in the environment. A security management plan will need to be implemented based on the assessment plan to include potential medical error, patent safety, mandatory federal regulations, current and future policy, and legislation that affects the field of health care. It is very important that a specific management plan is developed, implemented, and monitored.

Security management plans will stem from conducting an organization-specific security analysis to determine potential risks. The initial analysis will include the potential risks, the probabilities of security occurrences, the impact of the identified risks, what can be done to reduce or mitigate risks, and whether the risks can be avoided.

It is important that strategies are implemented in the health care environment, bearing in mind that the patient needs to take the center stage. Adequate training of the staff is crucial. Staff should avoid filling an expired patient prescriptions, ensure that test results are followed, track missed appointments, stress the importance of communicating with patients, prevent falls and increase mobility, and adequately retain records.

Security management includes patient readmission and safety.

Government Privacy Security

Government privacy security is the potential loss of control related to personal information (Grama 2019). This means that data need to be collected and carried out using an appropriate analysis. Organizations need to understand privacy risks to operate in business and consumer privacy law proposals. Information injuries that consist of deception, health and safety injuries, reputational injuries, and financial injuries need to be addressed appropriately using privacy security management. An example of typical deception would be a case of misleading with inaccurate claims on products. Another example that can be cited is health and safety injuries. This may be due to risks associated with privacy and data breaches.

Identification and minimized data protection security data are needed to carry out an appropriate assessment on privacy security. This means following standard process management that consists of cover notice, control access, correction, deletion, and portability. The concentration would be on individual control data. Product data from other client organizations will be collected.

Privacy Policies

The United States has state and federal level laws. This means organizations must have a privacy policy when collecting personal data (Cross Sector Data Sharing 2019). The laws are regulated by the Federal Trade Commission and specific clauses and provisions are required to ensure data privacy is in place.

There are approximately 80 countries that have legal development regulated privacy laws. The privacy framework consists of nine principles that make up privacy protections. Privacy protections address harm prevention, notice, collection limitation, use of personal information, choice, integrity of personal information, security safeguards, access and correction, and accountability.

The privacy policy must include clauses on third-party services, APIs, SDK, plugins, and other required items. Additionally, privacy policies must be posted on the organization's website. The website's privacy policy will detail personal information that is being collected from users, how the data are used, and how the data are kept private. Health Insurance Portability and Accountability Act (HIPAA) is included under the privacy rule and protects patients from unnecessary disclosures as health information is being collected.

Define General Data Protection Regulation (GDPR) Basics

Any individual or organization doing business in the European Union must understand the GDPR security standard (Hoofnagle, van der Sloot, and Borgesius 2019).

The GDPR was passed in the pre-Brexit era. Brexit is the potential or hypothetical departure of the United Kingdom from the European Union. The GDPR became enforceable on May 20, 2018. Collected and stored data must follow the standards regulated in GDPR. E-mail marketing has stricter consent regulations. Typical collected data include the following: e-mail, patient files, previous data consistent with stipulated rules and regulations, and advice to keep screenshots.

It is important to follow specific regulations when collecting data. This comes with options consent. Anyone collecting data should refrain from vague permissions rather than be explicit. The consent should be explicit with the e-mail provider level. Examples consist of the following:

- Advice to keep screenshots.
- All previous data should follow new rules.
- Files for noncompliance of the stipulated rules and regulations.
- Organizations should be careful with e-mail marketing.

Consequences for GDPR Noncompliance

GDPR affects any organization that does business with European Union organizations or individuals that collect and process personal data of

European citizens. The law requires that organizations dealing with such data need to comply with the GDPR law.

The United Kingdom Government and Information Commissioners Office has made it clear that there will be no new legislation to cover new and growing threats of cybercrime. Instead, the United Kingdom will enforce legislation about the use of data and the protection of personal data.

Noncompliant organizations will be fined. Some fines on certain articles of GDPR can be up to 20 million Euros or up to two percent of the total global revenue of the previous year based on which number is greater. The fines get the attention of organizations quickly. Noncompliance punishments go further than the monetary fines; cyberattacks can cost businesses from $14 to 2.35 million per incident and data breaches and attacks are growing all the time. Post-attack cost to brand and reputational damage is also possible. This can lead to business damage brand post attack.

Threat attacks on sensitive data are real. The magnitude of the attacks indicates that these threats to the Internet of things (IoT) are increasing. The IoT lacks adequate security due to its poorly protected data in legacy systems.

The most common of these regulations include the following:

GDPR aims to protect citizens in the European Union from data breaches. The GDPR applies to all companies processing personal data for people living in the European Union, even if that company is not physically located or based in the region.

HIPAA enforces several regulations about health care patients' data security. Any company that handles health care data such as hospitals, clinics, and insurance companies are required to comply with HIPAA regulations when handling data.

The Sarbanes-Oxley Act regulates compliance that involves maintaining financial records for seven years. This is required for U.S. company boards, management personnel, and accounting firms. The point of the regulation is to prevent another incident like the Enron scandal (D.M. 2018), which hinged on fraudulent bookkeeping.

FISMA treats information security as a national security entity for federal agencies. As part of the bill, all federal agencies are required to develop data protection methods.

PCI DSS is a set of regulations meant to help reduce fraud, primarily through protecting customer credit card information. PCI DSS security and compliance are required for all companies handling credit card information.

The Good Practice Guide 13 is the United Kingdom's GDPR for business processes. This system is implemented by many organizations and is compulsory for those managing high-impact data.

According to a recent CIO survey, the biggest compliance-related issues that organizations are currently facing are:

Bring Your Own Device is a personal mobile device that creates security vulnerabilities. Organizations can mitigate these issues through strong policies backed up by technical controls.

Following software updates and patching existing software when vulnerabilities are detected aids in software management.

Electronic Data Interchange (EDI) is the vendor management system. Major vulnerabilities come from EDI and vendor system integration. EDI allows organizations to send information in a standard format to other organizations electronically. This cuts out errors that occur when a paper approach is used. While some organizations use EDI, the latest trend is to use API with standard JavaScript Object Notation.

IoT end point vulnerabilities could lead to financial or reputational harm. Annual penetration testing should be used to make sure that IoT systems are compliant to security regulations.

Federal, state, and organizational regulations for data management:

Federal, state, and organizational regulations for data management address data retention and government public data, also known as open data.

The following is a list of some organizations and agencies that are responsible for creating data management regulations in different sectors. Organizations that are related to any field should comply to all the regulations of the agency dedicated to that field.

National Institute of Health:

- The organization must register clinical trials to comply with government regulations.
- Another regulation states that the research data must be retained for three years.
- Funded genomic research must develop a data sharing plan and submit data to a central repository so that sharing can be done easily between vendors. This creates a common repository to help build knowledge.

White House Mandates:

The White House mandate was issued by the White House Office of Science and Technology Policy under the direction of President Obama on February 22, 2013 (Nelson 2013). This mandate requires all granting agencies to establish a plan to make the results of federally funded research public and free of charge within one year after original publication. The following are several updates on this mandate after the original issue.

Here are some other agencies dealing with different fields, each having their own set of regulations.

- Department of Energy
- NASA
- Department of Defense
- Food and Drug Administration
- Department of Transportation

Data management varies based on the sector. It is always necessary to identify the sector so that the organization can follow the regulations and policies applicable to the associated agency.

- If the organization is in the medical sector, follow the regulations of the National Institute of Health.
- If the organization is in the energy sector, follow the regulations of the Department of Energy.

- If the organization is in food and drug items sector, follow the regulations of the Food and Drug Administration.

The updates are regularly posted on the government grants website and in the Office of Management and Budget. Organizations can also e-mail subscribe to get regular updates on changes in policies and regulations.

The following industries have influenced regulations:

- Tobacco industry
- Pharmaceutical industry
- Alcohol industry

Recent increases in legal regulations of information systems and data management have created a change, as data are not easily available. This requires an AI solution to keep up with the frequent changes. Organizations' research is mainly dependent on data. Data can be used to be the foundation of any research, but when data are scarce, the organization must comply with many regulations until it is time to retain the data.

Security Trends

Here are the security trend products available in the market (Kerner 2018; Kaur and Kaur 2018):

1. AlienVault: an AT&T company
2. BlackStratus focuses on SIEM (security information and event management) technology delivered on-premises and as a service
3. Dell Technologies, RSA (Rivest, Shamir, and Adelma—An example of asymmetric cryptography): NetWitness platform
4. Exabeam's security management platform
5. IBM QRadar security intelligence platform
6. Fortinet's fortiSIEM solution
7. LogPoint SIEM and LogPoint director software
8. ManageEngine's SIEM portfolio
9. McAfee's SIEM
10. Netsurion-EventTracker

11. Securonix SNYPR security analytics platform

12. SolarWinds log and event manager

13. Security intelligence platform

14. Venustech's SIEM solution

See Figure 6.1.

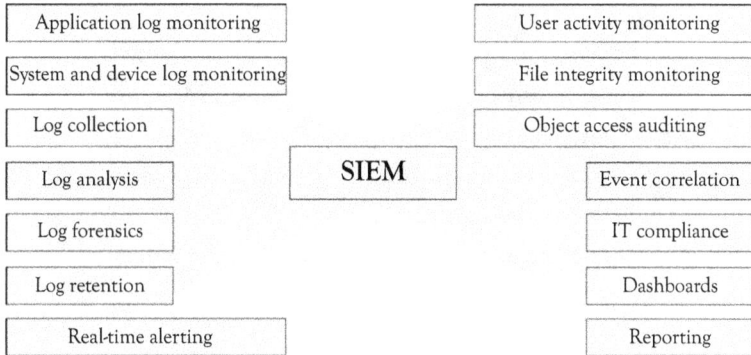

Figure 6.1 SIEM features in the security market

Countermeasures

Here are countermeasures that could help avoid security attacks:

- The system should have an access control mechanism that provides the privileges relevant to the role of the operations person.
- The system should have a single sign-on to access resources and the second layer of authentication on an individual resource.
- Create a decentralized logging system that allows a single login to access everything on the system and send notifications based on the filters.
- There should be an approval process in place.
- Implementing multilayered firewalls.
- Implementing multilayered authentication where users need to verify with user tokens that are generated every few seconds.

- Implement authentication on all systems in the network.
- No user should be given all the privileges on any system; instead, users should be restricted to the assets they have privileges on.
- Users who access the system from the outside should go through a secured and encrypted VPN.
- Restricting physical infrastructure through separating physical resources.
- Using a monitoring system that notifies others on any activities or assign someone to monitor the system. Monitoring the system automatically is effective and convenient.
- These countermeasures might stop attacks and metrics should be collected in the system quietly.
- Multilayered security can prevent attacks on the systems.

Vulnerability

A vulnerable system can be a problem for the owner of the system or an organization (Fiaidhi and Mohammed 2019). Vulnerability means the weakness of an asset that can be exploited by one or more attackers. In other words, it is a known issue that allows an attack to be successful. An example of this would be when a team member resigns and is not disabled from the system.

It is important to test for vulnerabilities to ensure the continued security of the systems by identifying weak points and developing a strategy to respond quickly. Here are some questions to ask when determining security vulnerabilities:

- Is the data backed up and stored in a secure off-site location?
- Is the data stored in the Cloud? If so, how exactly is it being protected from Cloud vulnerabilities?
- What kind of network security determines who can access, modify, or delete information from the organization system?
- What kind of antivirus protections are used? Are the licenses current? Is it running as often as needed?

- Is there data recovery plan in place? Is the event of a vulnerability being exploited? Understanding the vulnerabilities is the first step to managing system risks.

Important questions that need to be asked when it comes to security

The following questions must be asked by every organization:

- Is the company secure from security risks?
- Are the steps being done to protect the environment enough?
- Is the security being used adequate enough to protect the system?

Security

The following is a list of security risks that organizations face:

Disgruntled Staff: This happens when an employee—either current or former—tries to harm the organization. This may turn out to be a security issue if the employee feels unappreciated due to disrespectful treatment by the organization or company's other employees. Companies should implement data security so that employees cannot misuse administrative data to harm the company or its reputation.

Poorly Educated Employees: Another security issue emerges when an employee is not able to react to a security situation properly due to the bad training, or if the employee does not understand and follow the security policies to keep the organization safe.

Personal Devices: Everybody has a personal device that can be connected to the Internet. When an employee connects to the organization's secured network and come in contact with a virus contained link or website, it makes it easier for a hacker to hack into the system as one-layer security is already passed.

The Cloud: More security issues come when a company deals and works with the Cloud. An application that has been accessed through the Cloud can be accessed anywhere and anytime, which is very dangerous.

The virus can be implemented in any file and accessed by other employees, which leads to failure in the systems.

Outdated or Unpatched Devices: Another security issue comes from the use of outdated or unpatched devices like routers, printers, and servers that use firmware. Firmware must be updated to fight and remove the security containing threats. Even automatic updates bring the threats and risks to the system. Manual checks of patch updates have also resulted in failure, which means one attack can affect multiple systems.

Outsourcing: Third-party vendors and contractors who provide resources to the organization can also cause a security issue. While vendors and contractors provide many advantages to the organization—such as achieving targets and earning more profits—they also bring disadvantages. Many systems are remotely run by third-party vendors that have access and can steal personal data from the organization.

Security Solutions

Organization can use the following security solutions:

Disgruntled Staff: It is important to scan the system network daily for inactive privileged accounts. Accounts should be terminated and all the access should be revoked as soon as employees leave or get fired from the company to keep the system secure from this kind of risk.

Poorly Educated Employees: It is important to train all employees about possible security issues and teach them how to keep the system secure and safe from any kind of harm from external threats. It is also important to make sure that all the employees follow the company's security policies and contribute to keeping the organization environment safe and secure.

Personal Devices: The best solution is to implement network intrusion prevention and detection system in the organization's network to track and prevent any unauthorized access and activities. Organizations must implement a prevention system to ignore security from personal devices.

The Cloud: Cloud security can affect and attack multiple systems at the same time and bring big threats to the system. The solution to this kind of security is to implement the encryption and decryption techniques to save data from being hacked from a remote location. It is better to have something than nothing at all.

Outdated or Unpatched Devices: Automatic updates should be turned off; it is better to have patch management software scan all network devices. Patch management software will install and schedule new updates.

Outsourcing: A solution for outsourcing is to make sure the best practices are followed by the vendor when accessing remote data, and to make sure that the vendor's system is up to date with security needs and firewalls.

Cyber Strategy

The threat from cyberattacks is significant and continuously evolving. One estimate suggests cybercrime could cost businesses more than $2 trillion by 2019, nearly four times the estimated amount in 2015.

Cybersecurity Strategy Domain

See Figure 6.2.

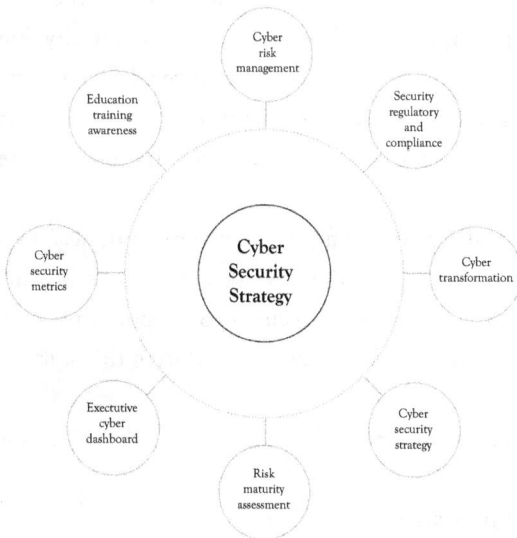

Figure 6.2 Cyber strategy with related features (Aliyeva and Gee-Hyun Hwang 2019)

Cyber Security Management

Organizations need to prepare for the worst-case scenario when it comes to security threats and breaches. Some of the threats are unforeseen. Developing cybersecurity management framework can safeguard the organization. The entities that can be included are as follows: cybersecurity remediation, treatment plans to report cyber risks, cybersecurity management framework, cybersecurity assessment methodology, and cybersecurity quantification.

Security Regulatory and Compliance

An organization has rules and regulations that need to be enforced. Local and international cybersecurity regulations and standards can be useful in making the security team be more alert when it comes to security issues.

Cyber Transformation

An organization's way of doing business is likely to change due to the utilization of digital Cloud connectivity, blockchain, and IoT. An organization that does not embrace the technology changes may find it hard to exist. This is likely to happen in the next decade. The introduction of technology into business will include Cloud, smart city, big data, IoT, blockchain, AI, and Fintech. It is likely there will be a shift in business strategy and approach. Using the Cloud may require using tools such as cryptography, isolation perimeter less, virtualization, multitenancy, and tokenization to control security.

Organizations are changing the way work is done. This means that employees want to access critical work applications anytime and anywhere. Applications should be secured to support this work approach. The following items should be considered during this shift:

- The shift away from traditional perimeter-based security and tools.
- A zero-trust security approach.
- A way of ensuring secure access to the Cloud and on-premises applications.

- Possibly use a zero-trust maturity model.
- Ensure there are adequate steps to efficiency and effective adaptation of a zero-trust security model in place.

Cybersecurity Strategy

A strategy is crucial when it comes to cybersecurity countermeasures. First, an organization must coin a good strategy that is going to work without failure. It is important that the organizations' management approves of the cybersecurity strategy proposed. The strategy must consist of objectives, missions, and a timeframe.

Cybersecurity Maturity Assessment

Some organizations may use the maturity model to help determine how well the security approach is working within the organization. Some organizations may choose not to use the maturity model. The maturity model is beneficial because it is ongoing, continuous, evolving, and helps measure the effectiveness of the process.

Executive Cyber Dashboard

It is helpful to use dashboard application to provide the security team with a glimpse at what is going on with security-related issues. A good approach is having a dashboard. It is helpful to have a cyber-community platform where threat issues are shared, providing transparency. The dashboard offers a platform for security teams and management to ask appropriate questions on cyber threats. This platform will also help train employees on cyber threats.

Cybersecurity Metrics

It is helpful for organizations to keep the metric of cybersecurity items (Mateski et al. 2012). These metrics will help the organization keep track of what is going on in terms of cyber threats. The cybersecurity teams can use the metrics to apply corrective actions and improve performance. It is a great idea to use regulatory and financial factors to meet requirements and measure IT security performance. Effective metrics help identify weaknesses, determine trends, and use resources to see success and failures in the security strategies and implementation.

Education, Training, and Awareness

The organization must train its employees on cybersecurity threats. Well-trained employees are an asset to the organization. Poorly trained employees become a weakness. The decision must be made by the management of the organization. Cybersecurity education, training, and awareness can be critical to the organization. These factors provide the workforce with adequate knowledge and methods to deal with cyber threats. Typically, there should be training on the following: identifying who can help with cyberattacks, what needs to be done, and who can help create efficient processes.

CHAPTER 7

Conclusion

Artificial Intelligence (AI) is becoming a phrase everywhere these days (Bridgwater 2018). You hear about AI on the television, radio, and the Internet. Security has been a topic in everyone's mind, and lack of security hurts organizations and individuals in the corporate world as well as domestically. Let us recap important reminders that will benefit all walks of life.

Security issues are not fun to experience. Organizations that have endured these predicaments do not take them lightly. Organizations should focus on security to avoid the negative impacts that come with security issues. Mitigations can be conducted in order to help with security issues.

It is important that security issues are identified early to minimize the impact of damages or fatal situation and there are many resources available. Security management is required to safely manage the situation. Data must be carefully collected; this may mean going through checklists to ensure appropriate questions are answered and that appropriate steps are taken based on those answers. This may include capturing historical data on security issues. Once accurate data are collected, the next step is to analyze the data carefully and accurately. Captured data may help predict the future security issues. This approach may help salvage nasty situations that can be damaging and expensive to the individual or organization.

Security issues come in many forms. Careful analysis will provide accurate direction for how to deal with each issue. AI has been chosen to provide the directions; however, data sources and quality of the data are crucial in every way. This book has provided various use cases that organizations can relate to. Organizations can utilize use cases to properly strategize the route to take. This leads to organizations defining, analyzing, monitoring, controlling, and mitigating risks and security.

Data science, data analytics, and machine learning (ML) algorithms are used to analyze data well that can ultimately help determine corrective actions. AI can carry out all the necessary determinations. Machines can learn from previous human experiences to enable continuous learning from new sets of input data based on the development of mathematical algorithms that led to the creation of ML. Complete AI system development is illustrated from data collection and shows how security data are processed with recommendations. Data collection and development offer the reader an understanding of how to tackle use cases such as AI, risk, and security in an organization. AI produces effective and dramatic results in business, and helps organizations improve security management skills.

Security has become important everywhere because of the large volume of data, different velocities, and variety of data stemming from various sources. This is illustrated and supported with case studies. Security concerns are growing bigger and more frequent with any amount of negative impact, and an undetermined positive security can hurt organizations when it comes to business opportunities, leading to loss of revenue. The range and breadth of security creates havoc everywhere in the world, and on a variety of projects. The importance of security management in organizations is shown in many sections of the book. The harm of security, without appropriate management and using the correct tools, can be devastating.

A lot of attention is given to problem statements with appropriate use cases and proposals of AI solutions using data science and ML. The comprehensive description of AI, risk, and security provides concrete answers to crucial questions that many organizations are struggling with: Where are these risks and what can be done to lower the impacts? Is AI part of the answer to security mitigation? Through answering these questions, organizations and individuals will gain a lot of knowledge and experiences.

This book can be used as a guide for organizations that are willing to create their own AI systems for security. Additionally, the reader can look at Bizstats.ai for more guidance. Numerous customized AI design tools are available at Bizstats.ai. The reader should feel free to contact Bizstats.ai should they need training on the tools used in the implementation of the AI.

References

5 steps to assess and mitigate cybersecurity risks. (n.d.). Retrieved from https://sungardas.com/en/about/resources/articles/5-steps-to-assess-and-mitigate-cyber-security-risks/

Anzilotti, E., J. Beer, L. Bell, J. Bernstein, A. Bluestein, K. Campbell-Dollaghan, and H. McCracken. 2019. "For Leading the Fbi to Its Biggest Ad-Fraud Bust Ever." *Fast Company*, no. 233, pp. 30–98.

Barylick, C. 2019. "CleanMyMac X 4.4.1 Review: Some Handy Tools But its Malware Detection Still Falls Short." *Macworld [Digital Edition]* 36, no. 8.

Berger, A.N., B. Imbierowicz, and C. Rauch. 2016. "The Roles of Corporate Governance in Bank Failures During the Recent Financial Crisis." *Journal of Money, Credit & Banking* 48, no. 729. doi: 10.1111/jmcb.12316

Berinato S. May 21, 2018. "Active Defense and "Hacking Back:" A Primer." *Harvard Business Review*. Retrieved from https://hbr.org/2018/05/active-defense-and-hacking-back-a-primer

Blass, G. 2019. "9 Steps for a Functional Compliance Program: How Health Care Organizations can Establish and Maintain Ongoing Security and Compliance Programs to Protect PHI." *Journal of Health Care Compliance* 21, no. 1, pp. 33–36.

Bolla, R., A. Carrega, and M. Repetto. February 18–21, 2019. Paper presented at "International Conference on Computing, Networking and Communications." doi: 10.1109/ICCNC.2019.8685665

Boland, M., and M. O'Riordan. 2019. "Preparedness and Management of Global Public Health Threats at Points of Entry in Ireland and the EU in the Context of a Potential Brexit." *Globalization & Health*, 15. doi:10.1186/s12992-019-0496-4

Bridgwater, A. 2018. "An Overview on Deep Learning Tools." *Computer Weekly*. Retrieved from https://computerweekly.com/news/252452432/An-overview-of-deep-learning-tools

Bronfman, N.C., P.C. Cisternas, P.B. Repetto, J.V. Castañeda. 2019. "Natural Disaster preparedness in a multi-hazard environment: Characterizing the Sociodemographic Profile of those Better (worse) Prepared." *PLoS ONE* 14, 1–18. doi:10.1371/journal.pone.0214249

Clark, P. April 1, 2019. "Look Forward, Not Backward to Fix FDIC's Flawed Brokered Deposit Rules." *American Banker*. Retrieved from https://americanbanker.com/opinion/look-forward-not-backward-to-fix-fdics-flawed-brokered-deposit-rules

Collins, J.C. 2019. "12 Common Technology Mistakes You Should Avoid." *Journal of Accountancy* 227, no. 1, pp. 1–7. Retrieved from https://journalofaccountancy.com/issues/2019/jan/common-technology-mistakes.html

Cooper, S. 2019. "9 Firms to Watch in AI Cybersecurity." *VPN News*. Retrieved from https://comparitech.com/blog/information-security/leading-ai-cybersecurity-companies/

de Vet, E., Eriksen, C., K. Booth, and S. French. 2019. "An Unmitigated Disaster: Shifting from Response and Recovery to Mitigation for an Insurable Future." *International Journal of Disaster Risk Science* 10, 179. doi: 10.1007/s13753-019-0214-0

Delaney, K. 2018. "AI and Security: The Arms Race." *Connected Futures: Executive Insights by Cisco*. Retrieved from https://connectedfutures.cisco.com/article/ai-security-arms-race/

Faiier, O., O. Arefieva, I. Miahkykh, N. Babko, S. Kuskova, and Khloponina-Gnatenko. 2019. "Risk Management in the Sphere of State Economic Security Provision Using Professional Liability Insurance." *Global Journal of Environmental Science and Management* 51, doi: 10.22034/gjesm.2019.05.SI.06

Fang, H., A. Qi, and X. Wang. 2019. "Fast Authentication and Progressive Authorization in Large-Scale IoT: How to Leverage AI for Security Enhancement?" *NSERC Discovery Program*.

Feldman, P. 2019. "Money, Time, and Management." *Contractor Magazine* 64, no. 2, p. 28. Retrieved from https://contractormag.com/feldmans/money-time-and-management-solutions

Fiaidhi, J., and S. Mohammed. 2019. "Security and Vulnerability of Extreme Automation Systems: The IoMT and IoA Case Studies." *IT Professional* 4, 48. doi:10.1109/MITP.2019.2906442

Freund, R.J., W.J. Wilson, and P. Sa. 2006. *Regression Analysis,* Vol. 2, AMsterdam: Academic Press. Retrieved from http://search.ebscohost.com/login.aspx?direct=true&AuthType=shib&db=nlebk&AN=320724&site=eds-live

Grama, Joanna Lyn, and Institute for Higher Education Policy (IHEP). 2019. "Protecting Privacy and Information Security in a Federal Postsecondary Student Data System. Protecting Students, Advancing Data: A Series on Data Privacy and Security in Higher Education." *Institute for Higher Education Policy*. Institute for Higher Education Policy. http://search.ebscohost.com/login.aspx?direct=true&AuthType=shib&db=eric&AN=ED595136&site=eds-live.

Hao, J., and T.K. Ho. 2019. "ML Made Easy: A Review of "Scikit-learn" Package in Python Programming Language." *Journal of Educational and Behavioral Statistics* 44, pp. 348–361. doi: 10.3102/1076998619832248

Hoofnagle C.J., B. van der Sloot, and F.Z. Borgesius, 2019. "The European Union General Data Protection Regulation: What It is and What

It Means." *Information & Communications Technology Law* 1, 65. doi: 10.1080/13600834.2019.1573501

Information Technology: Federal Laws, Regulations, and Mandatory Standards for Securing Private Sector Information Technology Systems and Data in Critical Infrastructure Sectors. 2008. *GAO-08-1075R.*

Infosec. October 18, 2018. "InfoSec World Turns 25, Brings Together Cybersecurity Stalwarts for Invigorating Discussions and Knowledge-Sharing [Press release]." Retrieved from https://infosecworldusa.com/2020/press-releases

Kastner, R., W. Hu, and A. Althoff. March 14–18, 2016. "Quantifying Hardware Security Using Joint Information Flow Analysis." Paper presented at the *2016 Design, Automation & Test in Europe Conference & Exhibition*, Dresden, Germany. IEEE.

Kaur, N., and I. Kaur. 2018. "Clean Technology: An Eagle-Eye Review on the Emerging Development Trends by Application of IOT Devices." Paper presented at *2018 IEEE International Conference on Smart Energy Grid Engineering (SEGE).* doi: 10.1109/SEGE.2018.8499518

Kerner, S.M. 2018. "AlienVault Integrates Endpoints into Unified Security Management." *eWeek.* Retrieved from https://eweek.com/security/alienvault-integrates-endpoints-into-unified-security-management

Kunkle F. April 30, 2019. "Cybersecurity is Significant Concern as Cars Become More Automated, Auto Industry Says." *The Washington Post.* Retrieved from https://washingtonpost.com/transportation/2019/04/30/auto-industry-says-cybersecurity-is-significant-concern-cars-become-more-automated/

Lankford, A., K.G. Adkins, and E. Madfis. 2019. "Are the Deadliest Mass Shootings Preventable? An assessment of Leakage, Information Reported to Law Enforcement, and Firearms Acquisition Prior to Attacks in the United States." *Journal of Contemporary Criminal Justice* 35, 315–341. doi: 10.1177/1043986219840231

Mannes, E., and C. Maziero. 2019. "Naming Content on the Network Layer: A Security Analysis of the Information-Centric Network Model." *ACM Computing Surveys,* 52, no. 3, pp. 1–28. doi: 10.1145/3311888

Mar, A. June 28, 2016. "130 Project Risks (List)." Retrieved from https://management.simplicable.com/management/new/130-project-risks

Mateski, M., C.M. Trevino, C.K. Veitch, J., Michalski, M. Harris, S. Maruoaka, and K. Frye. 2012. "Cyber Threat Metrics." *Sandia National Laboratories.* Retrieved from https://fas.org/irp/eprint/metrics.pdf

Mishchuk, E.V. 2018. "Enterprise Security Definition: Warranty Approach." *Vìsnik Žitomirs'kogo Deržavnogo Tehnologičnogo Unìversitetu Ekonomìčnì Nauki* 83, 83. doi: 10.26642/jen-2018-1(83)-83-89

Nelson, M., ed. 2013. *Guide to the Presidency and the Executive Branch,* 5th ed. Thousand Oaks, California, US: CQ Press.

Reddy, M. July 29, 2018. "The 3 Next Steps in Conversational AI." *Venture Beat.* Retrieved from https://venturebeat.com/2018/07/29/the-3-next-steps-in-conversational-ai/

Shaw, R., and A. Sharma. 2011. *Climate and Disaster Resilience in Cities.* Community, Environment and Disaster Risk Management. Bingley, UK: Emerald Group Publishing Limited. http://search.ebscohost.com/login.aspx?direct=true&AuthType=shib&db=e000xna&AN=362000&site=eds-live

Stafford, T., G. Deitz, and Y. Li. 2018. "The Role of Internal Audit and User Training in Information Security Policy Compliance." *Managerial Auditing Journal* 33, 410–424. doi: 10.1108/MAJ-07-2017-1596

Swire, P. 2018. "A Pedagogic Cybersecurity Framework: A Proposal for Teaching the Organizational, Legal, and International Aspects of Cybersecurity." *Communications of the ACM* 61, no. 10, 23–26. doi: 10.1145/3267354

Tan, A. 2018. "Key Considerations When Architecting a Smart City." *Telecom Asia*, pp. 6–9.

Umasuthan, V. May 3–5, 2016. "Protecting the Communications Network at Layer 2." Paper presented at *IEEE/PES Transmission and Distribution Conference and Exposition.* doi: 10.1109/TDC.2016.7519889

Walsh, L., S. Hill, M. Allan, S. Balandin, A. Georgiou, I. Higgins, and B. Hemsley. 2018. "A Content Analysis of the Consumer-Facing Online Information about My Health Record: Implications for Increasing Knowledge and Awareness to Facilitate Uptake and Use." *Health Information Management Journal* 47, no. 3, 106–115. doi: 10.1177/1833358317712200

Wang, T., Y. Wang, and C. Yen. 2019. "It's Not My Fault: The Transfer of Information Security Breach Information." *Journal of Database Management* 30, no. 3, 18–37. doi: 10.4018/JDM.2019070102

Watts, S. June 21, 2017. "IT Security Vulnerability vs Threat vs Risk: Understanding the Differences?" *BMC Blogs.* Retrieved from https://bmc.com/blogs/security-vulnerability-vs-threat-vs-risk-whats-difference/

Wells, J. 2019. "100 Companies that Matter in Knowledge Management." *KM World* 28, 12–17. Retrieved from http://kmworld.com/Articles/Editorial/Features/KMWorld-100-Companies-That-Matter-in-Knowledge-Management-2019-129903.aspx

Xue, D., J. Li, W. Wu, Q. Tian, & J. Wang. 2019. "Homology Analysis of Malware Based on Ensemble Learning and Multifeatures." *PLoS ONE*, 14, no. 8, 1–23. doi: 10.1371/journal.pone.0211373

About the Authors

Archie Addo

Consultant, coach, author, and program/project manager. Archie holds a PhD in Computer Information Systems (CIS) with an emphasis in e-commerce, cryptography, expert systems, and artificial intelligence. Dr. Addo has an Executive Data Science Certification from Johns Hopkins University, a certificate in Contract Law from Harvard Law School, Harvard University, Certified Project Management Professional (PMP), Certified ScrumMaster (CSM), and Certified Scrum Product Owner (CSPO). With more than 20 years of experience in interrelated disciplines, Archie works with computer science, project management, procurement, organizational design and development, process engineering, quality management, and project team facilitation. He has held management positions including Software Development Manager, Consultant, and Senior Project Manager.

Archie is a subject matter expert (SME) reviewer for Global Congress and India Congress Project Management Institute (PMI) and is a contributor to PMI Risk Standard Management.

Srini Centhala

Founder and Chief Architect of Absolut-e Data Com (a data company), providing expert consulting services to Fortune 100 companies (AT&T, Directv, Experian, eBay, and UPS) for more than 20 years and Chief Architect of BizStats Cloud Big Data AI Analytics platform. Centhala has designed and developed pricing engine, statistical modeling, prediction modeling, recommendation engine, text mining, sentiment analysis, data source analysis, and data science activities.

Specialties: Business process re-engineering, online business ideas, and concepts, business intelligence, technical architect/data architect/ data modeler in the business data management system, project management, and undertaking full projects, end to end. Srini applies machine learning and artificial intelligence to business data.

Muthu Shanmugam

Chief Technology Officer at Absolut-e Data Com with more than 20 years of experience in all phases of the software development lifecycle. Shanmugam holds a Master of Engineering from Anna University, India. He has worked with various enterprise organizations as a dynamic leader of software development teams. Currently, Muthu works on Bizstats. ai, a knowledge-base-powered business intelligence and analytics Cloud designed for businesses with limited BI resources. Key features include knowledge bases with numerous metrics and attributes for various industries, NLP-powered searches, dynamic reports, and dashboards. The company also features collaboration, which allows users to share reports and dashboards with their teams.

Index

Access control, 20–21
Access prevention, 52
Account takeover, 15
Accuracy, 77
  vs. epoch graph, 85
Advanced persistent threats, 15
Adware, 11
Akaike's information criterion
    (AIC), 92
Antivirus software, 44–45
Application cybersecurity, 43
Application security, 9–10, 19, 23,
    30, 35–36
Artificial intelligence (AI)
  approach, 69–72
  cybersecurity, 102–105
  design of, 2–3
  detect phase, 79–89
  discovery phase, 72–77
  evaluation, 77–79
  for federal cybersecurity, 62–63
  and human security, 59
  integrated system, 66
  machine learning and, 15–17,
    60–62
  mind map, 3–4
  monitor phase, 101–107
  protect phase, 99–100
  and security, 57–63
  start-up companies, 61–62
  threat response phase, 97–99
  threat score phase, 89–97
  transformation, 61
Assess management, 34
Asset discovery, 105
Audit reports, 52
Automobile industry, 111–112

Backdoor, 14
Backup software, 45
Bayes classifier, 86

Bayesian information criterion (BIC),
    92, 93
Bizstats.ai security knowledgebase,
    66–68
Bot, 14
Botnet, 14
Bots, 63
Bring Your Own Device, 116
Brute-force approach, 88
Business
  challenges, 6–7
  impacts and likelihoods, 47–48
  and security, 17–18

Check Point, 103
Cloud, 121–123
Cloud security, 10, 19
Communication security, 18
Confusion matrix, 77–78, 84
Content security, 37
Continuous monitoring and
    assessment, 33
Countermeasures, 46, 119–120
Credit security management,
    110–111
Critical information, 45
Cross-validation approach, 86, 88
Cross-validation comparison, 94
Cryptographic security, 18
Cryptomining/cryptojacking, 12
CSO, 63
Cyberattacks, 60
Cyber criminals, 62–63
Cyber dashboard, 125
Cybersecurity, 6, 10, 29, 102–105
  application security, 30, 35–36
  artificial intelligence for, 62–63
  categories, 42–43
  data security, 30, 34–35
  education, training, and awareness,
    126
  endpoint security, 30, 36–38

maturity assessment, 125
metrics, 125–126
network security perimeter security,
    30, 38–41
operations, 29, 32–33
perimeter security, 31, 41–42
prevention, 28, 31–32
standards, 49
strategy, 125
Cyber security management, 124
Cyber strategy, 123–126
Cyberterrorism, 6
Cyber threats intelligence, 31
Cyber transformation, 124–125
Cylance, 103
Cynet, 103

DAR, 34
Darktrace, 102
Data and drive encryption, 35
Database and monitoring scanning,
    36
Database secure gateway, 36
Data classification, 34–35
Data in motion, 34
Data integrity management, 35
Data link cybersecurity, 42–43
Data protection, 63
Data security, 9, 21–23, 30, 34–35
Data wiping and cleansing, 34
Deep neural network, 90–92
Denial-of-service (DoS) attacks, 15,
    39, 43
Desktop firewall, 36–37
Detect phase, 71, 79–89
DHS Einstein, 42
Digital forensics, 33
Disaster security management, 110
Discovery phase, 70, 72–77
Disgruntled staff, 121, 122
Distributed denial of service, 15
DIU, 34
DLP, 35, 38, 41, 42
Dynamic application testing, 36

Educated employees, 121, 122
Electronic access control, 20
Electronic Data Interchange (EDI), 116

Emission security, 18
Employees, organization, 52
Employee training, 23
Enclave and datacenter firewall, 38
Endpoint detection and response,
    106–107
Endpoint security, 30, 36–38
Ensemble classifier class, 87
Enterprise message security, 40–41
Enterprise remote access, 41
Enterprise right management, 34
Environmental monitoring, 23
Environmental security, 6
Escalation management, 33
Exploit, 13, 14

Federal desktop core compliance,
    37–38
Federal Information Security
    Management Act (FISMA),
    6, 116
Federal, state, and organizational
    regulations, 116–117
Financial management, 110–111
Firebird, 36
FireEye, 103
Focus operations, 33
Forensic process, 33
Fortinet, 103

General Data Protection Regulation
    (GDPR), 114–116
Government privacy security, 113

Health Insurance Portability and
    Accountability Act (HIPAA),
    6, 114, 115
Health security, 6
Health security management,
    112–113
Honeypot, 42
Human intelligence, 65
Human security and AI, 59
Human threats, 97

Identification, 34
Incendiary speech, 15

Incidence reporting, detection, response, 33
Industry domain
  automobile, 111–112
  credit and financial management, 110–111
  cyber strategy, 123–126
  disaster, 110
  government privacy security, 113
  health security management, 112–113
  insurance, 109–110
  privacy policies, 113–118
  security trend, 118–123
Information security, 8–10, 19, 27–28, 44
Information security policy, 25–27
Information systems security, 50
Infrastructure security, 10
Inline patching, 40
Insurance security management, 109–110
Intelligently secure conditional access, 59
Internet, 15–16
Internet of things (IoT), 115, 116
Internet security, 20
Intrusion detection system (IDS), 21, 37, 39, 41, 105
Intrusion Prevention System (IPS), 21, 37, 39, 41
ISO/IEC 27002–2005, 50
IT security, 8, 31

J.P. Morgan security, 6

Keylogger, 12, 15
Knowledgebase, 65–68
Knowledge sharing, 67–68

Linux, 36–37
Local area network, 7
Local Directory Access Protocol, 21
Locked doors, 22–23
Logical access, 20
Login attack, 15
Login ID, 28
Logistic regression, 86

Machine learning (ML), 15–17, 60–62, 66, 106
Malicious cryptomining, 12
Malware, 10–15, 17, 27
Malware infection, 13
Management security, 9, 43–45
Mean square error (MSE), 77
Message security, 41–42
Mitigation, security, 6–7, 23, 46–48
Mobile security, 19–20
Monitor phase, 71–72, 101–107
Multiple regression, 92

National Institute of Health, 117
Natural Language Processing (NLP), 74
Network access control, 40
Network cybersecurity, 43
Network metadata extracted features, 73
Network operations center, 32
Network security, 18–20, 22
Network security perimeter security, 30, 38–41
Network threat detection technology, 101
Neural network layers, 91

Operational security, 43, 45–46
Operational standards, 48–53
Ordinary least squares (OLS), 92
Organizational security, 51
Organization, employees, 52
Outdated/unpatched devices, 122, 123
Outsourcing, 122, 123

Password, 24, 28
Patch management, 38
Pattern-based learning, 66
Payment Card Industry Data Security Standard (PCI DSS), 49, 116
Perimeter firewall, 41
Perimeter security, 31, 41–42
Personal devices, 121, 122
Personnel security, 18
Phishing (aka masquerading), 15
Physical access, 20

Physical cybersecurity, 42
Physical intrusion detection, 23
Physical security, 6, 18, 19, 22–23, 44, 53–55, 60
Policy users, 25
Precision–recall curves, 84–85
Presentation cybersecurity, 43
Privacy policies, 113–118
Protect phase, 71, 99–100
Public key infrastructure, 34

Random forest classifier, 86
Ransomware, 12, 17
Reaper and IoTroop, 63
Receiver operating characteristic (ROC) curve, 76–77
Response and remediation plan, 52–53
Rootkit, 12
Root mean square error (RMSE), 94, 95
R-squared comparison graph, 93

Sarbanes-Oxley Act, 115
Scanning, 14
Scoring methods, 77
Secured equipment, 23
Secure DMZ, 41
SecureLink, 41
Security. See also Cybersecurity
    application, 23
    architecture and design, 32
    artificial intelligence and, 57–63
    assessment, 46
    awareness training, 32
    and business, 17–18
    controls, 20–21
    dashboard, 33
    defined, 5–6, 8
    information, 8–10, 27–28
    information and event management, 33
    knowledgebase, 66–68
    malware, 10–15, 27
    management, 32, 43–45
    mitigations, 6–7, 23, 46–48
    ML and AI, 15–17
    monitoring, 101
    network, 22
    operation, 45–46
    operations center, 32
    physical, 22–23, 53–55
    policy compliance training, 52
    regulatory and compliance, 124
    responses, 48
    risk, 121–122
    solutions, 122–123
    standards and policies, 7–8, 24–27, 48–53
    threats, 9
    trend, 118–123
    types of, 18–21
Security Assertion Markup Language, 21
Sensors, 7
Service level object, 33
Session cybersecurity, 43
SIEM, 118–119
SLA, 33
Sniffing, 15
Social engineering, 15
Sophos, 103
Spam, 15
Spear phishing, 15
Spyware, 11
Static application review, 35–36
Sustainable security, 51
Symantec, 103
System software, 44

Threat assessment, 45
Threat modeling, 31–32
Threat response phase, 71, 97–99
Threats, 47, 51–52
Threat score phase, 71, 89–97
Transmission security, 18
Transportation cybersecurity, 43
Trojan and Trojan Horse, 11–12

User domains, 7
Utility software, 44

Vectra, 103–104
Vendor system integration, 116
Virtual Private Network (VPN), 7

Virus, 11
VoIP Protection, 39–40
Vulnerability, 120–121
  analysis, 46–47
  assessment, 32
  management, 10

WAF, 36
Wannacry attack, 18

Web proxy content filtering, 40
Weighted average calculation, 87
White House mandate, 117–118
Wide area network, 7
Workstations, 7
Worms, 11, 62

Zero-day vulnerability, 15
Zombie, 62